OECD Green Growth Studies

Towards Green Growth?

TRACKING PROGRESS

This work is published under the responsibility of the Secretary-General of the OECD. The opinions expressed and arguments employed herein do not necessarily reflect the official views of OECD member countries.

This document and any map included herein are without prejudice to the status of or sovereignty over any territory, to the delimitation of international frontiers and boundaries and to the name of any territory, city or area.

Please cite this publication as:
OECD (2015), *Towards Green Growth?: Tracking Progress*, OECD Green Growth Studies, OECD Publishing, Paris.
http://dx.doi.org/10.1787/9789264234437-en

ISBN 978-92-64-23441-3 (print)
ISBN 978-92-64-23443-7 (PDF)

${periodicity}: OECD Green Growth Studies
ISSN 2222-9515 (print)
ISSN 2222-9523 (online)

The statistical data for Israel are supplied by and under the responsibility of the relevant Israeli authorities. The use of such data by the OECD is without prejudice to the status of the Golan Heights, East Jerusalem and Israeli settlements in the West Bank under the terms of international law.

Photo credits: Cover © design by advitam for the OECD.

Corrigenda to OECD publications may be found on line at: *www.oecd.org/about/publishing/corrigenda.htm*.

FOREWORD

Four years after the launch of the OECD Green Growth Strategy, this report draws lessons from country experience and examines how to enhance policy design to deliver green growth.

***Towards Green Growth? Tracking Progress* takes stock of country experience in implementing green growth since 2011.** The 2011 OECD Green Growth Strategy provided important first guidance to governments on how to implement green growth by fostering economic growth and development, while ensuring that natural assets continue to provide the resources and environmental services vital to human well-being. Green growth implies transforming current modes of production and consumption across the entire economy at a global scale so as not to simply displace unsustainable production and consumption patterns. This report assesses common challenges experienced by OECD countries and partner economies since 2011 in aligning economic and environmental priorities for green growth. It seeks to accelerate progress by highlighting where there is scope to heighten the ambition and effectiveness of green growth policy in order to help countries seize available opportunities.

Revisiting the Green Growth Strategy to increase well-being. Recognising green growth policy design as work in progress, the 2011 Green Growth Strategy recommended further effort in a number of areas: carrying out further analysis of innovation and investment policies, where asymmetric information poses serious challenges; considering the role of social policies to help compensate potential losers and reduce labour market disruption resulting from the structural transformation; integrating green growth into core OECD policy advice to account for country-specific circumstances; and advancing the development of relevant indicators to measure progress. Accordingly, OECD green growth analysis has deepened since 2011. This report surveys the work undertaken over the last four years across the many disciplines relevant to green growth. It considers the extent to which the Green Growth Strategy can be reviewed and strengthened, both by the analysis performed and the lessons learnt from country challenges in implementing policy to date.

Institutional processes for mainstreaming green growth are also vital to progress. The OECD has made a concerted and sustained effort to integrate green growth across its work programme; its experience shows that institutional settings matter. Significant progress has been made in the mainstreaming process, as shown by the volume of work undertaken since 2011. Yet progress is uneven, and important areas for further work remain. To implement effective green growth strategies, governments must drive institutional changes to integrate economic and environmental decision-making, as well as ensure co-ordination across core policy areas similar to those being implemented by the OECD. Thus, governments and other organisations trying to implement green growth may learn from the mainstreaming experience of the OECD.

The ultimate aim of this report is to accelerate countries' implementation of green growth policies by providing more targeted and coherent policy advice. The guidance emerging from country experience, the enriched Green Growth Strategy and lessons learnt from the OECD mainstreaming process are intended to serve as tools to this end. The report will help target future policy advice by highlighting priority areas for further analysis and opportunities to enhance mainstreaming at the OECD and beyond. The Green Growth Strategy frames OECD work on the environment, as an integral part of promoting broader measures of prosperity that fully recognise the role of natural capital in economic growth and human well-being. As such, the report forms part of the Organisation's broader input to major environmental policy milestones, including the United Nations Conference on Climate Change and negotiation of the Post-2015 development agenda, as well as environmental work being undertaken in the context of other international forums, such as the G20.

NAVIGATING THIS REPORT

The Executive Summary covers main findings and recommendations for policy makers.

Taking stock of four years of the Green Growth Strategy...

1 Outlines principal elements of the 2011 Green Growth Strategy.

2 Outlines lessons from country challenges in implementing green growth policy frameworks.

...to take the green growth agenda forward.

3 Updates the Green Growth Strategy in light of OECD work and country experience since 2011, and puts forward next steps for consideration.

4 Reviews progress in mainstreaming and considers how to accelerate the process, highlighting lessons for both the OECD and governments.

ACKNOWLEDGEMENTS

This report is an output of the OECD Horizontal Programme on Green Growth, overseen by Catherine Mann (Chief Economist) and Simon Upton (Director, Environment Directorate). Its elaboration has drawn upon the OECD's expertise with economics and environment policies, indicators and measures of progress. It has been prepared in co-operation with the Economics Department (ECO), the International Energy Agency (IEA), the Directorate for Financial and Enterprise Affairs (DAF), the Directorate for Science, Technology and Innovation (STI), the Development Cooperation Directorate (DCD), the Statistics Directorate (STD), the Public Governance and Territorial Development Directorate (GOV) and the Trade and Agriculture Directorate (TAD).

This report was prepared and led by Justine Garrett, with co-author Ryan Parmenter, from the Green Growth Unit, under the supervision of Nathalie Girouard (former Green Growth Co-ordinator, now Head, *Environmental Performance and Information Division, Environment Directorate*). Thanks to Rachel Samson of Carist Consulting for drafting inputs, Lupita Johanson for communication support, and to interns Sven Van Mourik (*American University of Paris*) and Florian Egli (*The Graduate Institute*, Geneva). Deborah Holmes-Michel provided invaluable administrative support.

This report has benefitted from consultation with the following OECD bodies: Economic and Development Review Committee (EDRC), Economic Policy Committee Working Party 1 (EPC/WP1), Environment Policy Committee (EPOC), Working Party on Integrating Environmental Policies (EPOC/WPIEEEP), Working Party on Climate, Investment and Development (EPOC/WPCID), Committee on Statistics and Statistical Policy (CSSP), Committee for Scientific and Technology Policy (CSTP), Investment Committee (IC), Development Assistance Committee Network on Environment and Development Co-operation (DAC/ENVIRONET), Committee on Industry, Innovation and Entrepreneurship (CIIE), Joint Meeting of Tax and Environment Experts (JMTEE), Working Party on Environmental Information (WPEI) and the Working Party on Biodiversity, Water and Ecosystems (WPBWE).

The authors are grateful to Janine Treves, Katherine Kraig-Ernandes, and Romy de Courtay who assisted with publication and editing as well as *Lokaalwerk* (Ernst Bernson and Yvonne Willems) who developed the visual elements and layout of the report.

TABLE OF CONTENTS

TABLES

FIGURES

BOXES

RECURSOS PESQUEROS
PLANIFICACIÓN URBANA
ENVIRONMENTAL R
INSTRUMENTS DE MARCHÉ
MARCHÉS DU TRAVAIL
ÉCOSYSTÈMES
ÉMISSIONS DE CO_2, SO_x, NO_x
COMPETENCIAS
INNOVACIÓN
GOBERNANZA
ÉDUCATION ENVIRONNEMENTALE
COÛT DE L'INACTION
VERTE
INFRASTRUCTURE
WILDLIFE RESOURCES
ELECTRICIDAD
DÉVELOPPEMENT DURABLE
R&
ENERGY INTENSITY
INDICADORES
INVESTMENT AND FINANCE
DESECHOS
CAMBIO CLIMÁTICO
EDIFICIOS ECOLÓGICOS
FIRM BEHAVIOUR
MULTIFACTOR PRODUCTIVITY
FORMACIÓN
ESTRATEGIAS DEL CRECIMIE TO VERDE
ENVIRONMENTAL GOODS AND SER
IMPACT SUR LES MÉNAGES
RESSOURCE DU SOL
FLUX DE MATIÈRES
PRODUCIÓN DEL CO^2

LAND COVER
PATRIMOINE NATUREL
ACCORDS INTERNATIONAUX
PATENTS
RISQUE SYSTÉMIQUE
FRESHWATER RESOURCES
CIUDADES ECOLÓGICAS
BIODIVERSITY LABELLING
ENERGY PRODUCTIVITY
RESSOURCES MINÉRALES
SOCIAL POLICY
POLICY POLÍTICAS LOCALES
CO-ORDINATION
SANTÉ
SUBSIDY REFORM
WATER POLLUTION PRICING
EFFETS SUR LA COMPÉTITIVITÉ
LANDFILL WASTE
REGULACIÓN
GREEN SUBSIDIES
USOS DEL SUELO
FIRM BEHAVIOUR
FOSSIL FUELS
DÉVELOPPEMENT
QUALITÉ DE VIE
AGRICULTURA
COMERCIO
POLLUTION ATMOSPHÉRIQUE
RESOURCE PRODUCTIVITY
FINANZAS INTERNACIONALES
MARCHÉS
SUBVENCIONES ECOLÓGICAS
FOREST RESOURCES
MESURES VOLONTAIRES
CONSUMER BEHAVIOUR
ADAPTACIÓN
PLANIFICATION RÉGIONALE
PRODUCTOS QUÍMICOS
OPPORTUNITÉS D'EMPLOI
AGUA
PRODUCTIVITÉ MATÉRIELLE
EMISSIONS TRADING
TAXATION
RESOURCE BOTTLENECKS
AGUA POTABLE
ECOTURISMO
TRANSPORTE
SEWAGE TREATMENT
TRAFFIC CONGGESTION
ENERGY PRICING
SYSTÈME FISCAL
PRIX DU CARBONE
TECNOLOGÍA
ACCÈS À L'ÉNERGIE

EXECUTIVE **SUMMARY**

KEY FINDINGS AND RECOMMENDATIONS

121

billion USD government spending on renewable energy subsidies, 2013

60

jurisdictions with or considering carbon pricing

2%

average share of GDP from environmentally-related taxes, OECD countries

3

pillars of growth: productivity growth, green growth, inclusive growth

42

signatory countries to the OECD Declaration on Green Growth

4%

GDP average social cost of outdoor air pollution, OECD countries

COUNTRIES ARE TAKING STEPS TOWARDS GREEN GROWTH, YET MUCH MORE DETERMINED EFFORTS ARE NEEDED TO INTEGRATE ENVIRONMENTAL PRIORITIES INTO ECONOMIC AGENDAS.

The 2011 Green Growth Strategy: "Green" and "growth" must go hand-in-hand. In 2009, OECD ministers asked the OECD to develop a Green Growth Strategy to help the governments of OECD countries and partner economies alike achieve economic recovery, along with environmentally and socially sustainable growth. The 2011 Green Growth Strategy responded to this mandate: it sets a framework for governments to foster economic growth and development, while ensuring that natural assets continue to provide the resources and environmental services vital to human well-being. It recognises that risks to growth continue to rise as traditional growth models negatively affect the physical environment that ultimately underpins human well-being. In addition to the need for greater productivity growth, a growth agenda must take account of the consequences of productivity growth for the supporting physical environment. The need to ensure that growth is inclusive is a further pillar for growth.

Four years on, governments have taken steps towards green growth. Most countries have implemented some measures to begin pricing pollution and provide incentives for efficient resource use, such as pricing instruments, regulatory measures and subsidies. Around one-third of OECD countries and a number of OECD partner economies have adapted, or are adapting, the Green Growth Strategy's indicator framework to help evaluate and monitor progress towards national green growth objectives.

Much more concerted efforts are needed to meaningfully align economic and environmental priorities. To drive green growth, governments must embed environmental challenges at the heart of economic policy making, by linking environmental and economic reform priorities in a consistent set of objectives. Finance and economic ministries have a major role to play. A number of countries have taken relevant measures, including developing green growth strategies and inter-ministry committees co-ordinating elements of green growth policy. Yet no country has comprehensively linked environmental and economic reform priorities. Measurability also remains a challenge, as many countries lack data over sufficient time periods to enable effective assessment of policies.

OECD advice since 2011 demonstrates that the transition remains a work in progress. Since 2011, the OECD has integrated green growth considerations into their core policy advice to countries. The most commonly identified challenges include establishing an explicit price on carbon; implementing pricing instruments for water, waste and transport; shifting the tax burden in favour of environmentally related taxation; and eliminating environmentally harmful discrepancies in tax systems. Further challenges include managing subsidies to promote green technologies; phasing out environmentally perverse subsidies; and gearing sectoral policy to support green growth in areas such as infrastructure, innovation and energy efficiency. The challenges are not exhaustive, and will not necessarily apply to all countries, but they demonstrate where main opportunities to improve the effectiveness of green growth policy implementation lie across countries.

A much better understanding of the opportunities and trade-offs of green growth policies is fundamental to progress. If governments do not have a clear grasp of the economic opportunities created by environmental policy – or the potential feedbacks of environmental damages on gross domestic product growth – they will struggle to align economic and environmental priorities to establish green growth objectives. Important analysis has emerged since 2011, but much more work is needed to demonstrate both the economic opportunities and improved environmental outcomes of policies designed to enhance green growth (e.g. work to further understanding of the broader economic effects of environmental policies such as on investment, production processes, firm entry-exit, and work to quantify feedbacks of environmental damage on economies). As an integral part of promoting broader measures of prosperity that fully recognise the role of natural capital in economic growth and human well-being, such efforts can also help inform relevant international negotiations, such as the United Nations Conference on Climate Change, negotiation of the post-2015 development agenda, and environmental work being undertaken in the context of the G20.

GOVERNMENTS SHOULD

- depart **from "business as usual" policies that do not account for environmental costs and implement green growth policies, recognising that economic and environmental performance are inseparable in the long run.**
- advance **understanding of the complementarities and trade-offs between economic and environmental goals, to better inform economic and environmental reform priority-setting.**

PUBLIC TRUST IS A CENTRAL PILLAR FOR REFORM: GOVERNMENTS MUST NURTURE IT

Direct pricing of environmentally harmful activity is indispensable to green growth, but political opposition is a fundamental challenge. Although it is more economically efficient to tax externalities directly, opposition to such measures means that taxing the inputs or outputs of environmentally damaging activities, such as motor vehicle fuels or electricity, remains far more prevalent than explicit pricing mechanisms.

Country experience demonstrates that green growth is likely to continue to encounter political opposition without more concerted effort to tackle the political challenges associated with reform. Further policy experimentation is needed, with rigorous ex post evaluation and rapid dissemination of results through, for instance, case studies. Experience in jurisdictions such as Ireland and the Canadian province of British Columbia show that leadership, consultation, incremental implementation and transparent analysis can contribute to successful implementation of pricing mechanisms.

Where constituencies are strongly opposed to tax increases or shifts, governments may need to consider policy mechanisms other than direct pricing. Implicit pricing and regulatory approaches may be more effective means to implement and help advance progress.

Potential distributional consequences, including labour market and household impacts, merit greater policy focus. Policy support for overall labour market mobility and skill development should be responsive to demand, and training programmes should be continuously adjusted to changing employer demands. As more jobs require more green skills, existing labour and social policy systems should accommodate that shift, just as they adjusted to the demands of rapidly expanding information and communications technologies. Ensuring an effective social safety net is particularly important in developing countries, where populations may be more vulnerable to impacts associated with reform, and transfer systems are less developed or non-existent. In addition to helping ease reform, such measures are essential to ensuring that green growth policy does not exacerbate inequality, which is already on the rise in many countries.

40% of OECD country surveillance since 2011 makes recommendations on carbon pricing

10% of country surveillance alone consider household implications

17% of country surveillance alone consider labour market impacts

GOVERNMENTS SHOULD

- place **greater emphasis on political challenges associated with green growth reform, particularly implementation of direct pricing mechanisms, drawing on country experience (e.g. ex post evaluation of policies and case studies)**
- consider **more active pursuit of regulatory approaches where constituencies are strongly against tax increases or shifts**
- advance **understanding of how significant regressive effects of environmental policy are likely to be on households and identify emerging best practices from experience to date, including from a political-economy perspective**
- ensure **that policy support for general labour market mobility and skill development is responsive to demand generated by green growth, and continuously adjust training programmes to changing employer demands. As more jobs require more green skills, existing labour and social policy systems should accommodate this shift.**

MISALIGNMENTS IN GOVERNMENT POLICY ACT AS A MAJOR IMPEDIMENT TO REFORM

Green growth depends on strong, coherent signals that the costs of environmental degradation and unsustainable resource use will gradually increase. Regulatory action to gear existing sectoral and issue-specific policy towards supporting green growth is also essential. Current government policy is not consistent when it comes to helping shift producer and consumer behaviour to support green growth.

Governments globally continue to spend USD 640 billion (US dollars) per year on environmentally harmful fossil-fuel subsidies, in direct contradiction with green growth goals. Support to fossil-fuel consumers, predominantly in developing and emerging economies, reached an estimated USD 548 billion in 2013, more than four times the amount spent on renewable energy. Support for both consumption and production in OECD countries varied between USD 55-90 billion from 2005 to 2011. Fossil-fuel subsidies continue to serve as a major impediment to green growth, shoring up the role of incumbent polluting technologies, holding back investment in cleaner emerging technologies, and acting as a negative price on carbon.

The structure and level of taxes on energy use are not environmentally coherent in many OECD countries. There are inconsistencies in the taxation of different forms, uses and users of energy when assessed against environmental and other social costs, for which the rationale is not obvious. For example, diesel fuel is taxed at lower rates than gasoline both in terms of energy and carbon content in 33 out of 34 OECD countries, despite the fact that on a per litre basis, diesel emits higher levels of harmful local air pollutants and carbon dioxide. This demonstrates broad scope for governments to align policies in support of green growth. Work undertaken since 2011 demonstrates that current government policy is not supportive enough to accelerate green infrastructure investment or green innovation, for example.

If policies within sectors are not coherent from an environmental perspective, the potential for inconsistency across policy areas is even greater. Recent work on policy alignment for the transition to a low-carbon economy supports this proposition. Climate policy interacts with policies in many

548

billion USD support for fossil fuel consumers in developing and emerging economies, 2013 (4 times renewable energy support)

55-90

billion USD support for consumption and production of fossil fuels, OECD countries, 2005-2011

26.8

billion EUR fiscal cost per year due to favourable tax treatment of company cars; 116 EUR associated social costs areas, as almost all economic activities generate greenhouse gas emissions. The result can be frictions, unintended consequences or conflicts in policy objectives. Several misalignments currently act as obstacles to the transition. These include cross-cutting economic policy domains – investment, taxation, innovation and international trade – as well as policies governing specific areas that are critical to the low-carbon transition, such as electricity systems, urban mobility and rural land use.

GOVERNMENTS SHOULD

- re-invigorate **efforts to eliminate fossil-fuel subsidies, as a basic policy measure for green growth**
- review **the coherency of sectoral policy from a green growth perspective, both within and across sectors.**

ONGOING DATA COLLECTION IS NEEDED TO EVALUATE AND MONITOR THE TRANSITION TOWARDS GREEN GROWTH

Green growth indicator development requires progress on two fronts: developing methodologies and addressing data gaps. Green growth indicators continue to be developed, including six headline indicators intended to help articulate and monitor central elements of green growth. Progress in this field must be matched by country efforts to guarantee data availability and quality, to ensure that a lack of good data does not hamper indicator production and use, and to support efforts to track progress. The role of national statistics agencies is vital, as measurability remains a challenge for many countries.

GOVERNMENTS SHOULD

- accelerate **efforts to ensure data availability and quality in priority areas such as internationally comparable, environmental-economic accounts (e.g. accounts of air emissions and natural resources) and data on the state of the environment (e.g. biodiversity and ecosystem health, and air and water quality), while continuing efforts to advance indicator methodologies.**

MAINSTREAMING IS PROCEEDING AT A RAPID PACE AT THE OECD, BUT PROGRESS IS UNEVEN; INSTRUCTIVE LESSONS ARISE FOR BOTH GOVERNMENTS AND THE ORGANISATION

Institutional settings matter. The OECD has made a concerted and sustained effort to integrate green growth across its work programme, to good effect: around 70% of country policy surveillance in the four core areas of relevance *(Economic Surveys, Environmental Performance Reviews, Investment Policy Reviews and Reviews of Innovation Policy)* now contain green growth recommendations. Yet overall progress masks considerable differences across publication series and green growth issues. To drive green growth, governments should implement institutional changes to integrate economic and environmental decision-making and ensure co-ordination across relevant ministries that are similar to those undertaken by the OECD to ensure coherence in its work programme. Lessons from the OECD process are therefore relevant for governments and other organisations seeking to implement green growth.

26

green growth indicators, 2011 Green Growth Strategy

6

headline indicators to raise awareness, measure progress, identify opportunities and risks

Drawing lessons from success. Green growth recommendations are included in around 82% of Economic Surveys, which are driving the overall high rate of green growth advice in OECD country surveillance, along with Environmental Performance Reviews. A number of mechanisms have driven the relatively rapid rate of progress. The most important elements include: high-level leadership and clear accountabilities; formal structures for co-ordination and collaboration; clear articulation of how green growth links to other policy priorities (e.g. in an overarching analytical framework that situates green growth alongside other overarching government objectives); and dedicated human resources for the mainstreaming process. Ensuring mechanisms to encourage information sharing across policy areas and promoting measurable indicators for use in policy analysis are also important.

GOVERNMENTS SHOULD

- assess **and fine-tune institutional settings for green growth mainstreaming, potentially taking OECD experience as an example**
- initiate **the culture change (e.g. strategic oversight at the highest levels of government; mechanisms to drive co-operation between relevant ministries; and leadership role for economic policy makers as well as environment ministries) required to engage economic and other relevant ministries in addressing green growth-related issues.**

NEXT STEPS: ENRICHING GREEN GROWTH ADVICE

The conclusions of this report suggest a number of forward work priorities for governments, the OECD and other relevant institutions to support government implementation efforts. Work to enhance understanding of complementarities and trade-offs between economic and environmental goals; enhancing public trust in green growth; and ensuring that environmental policies are coherent and aligned across sectors are priority areas. Further developing and making use of headline indicators to raise awareness, measure progress and identify opportunities and risks is also essential, as is work on the ocean economy and mining in gearing sectoral policies for green growth. These areas merit particular consideration from governments, but do not detract from the need to consider the full suite of measures outlined in the Green Growth Strategy in implementing reform.

GOVERNMENTS SHOULD

- advance **the forward work priorities identified in this report to help accelerate green growth implementation efforts**
- support **the mainstreaming of the Green Growth Strategy across OECD Committees' work according to the identified priorities.**

70%

of OECD country surveillance since 2011 contains green growth recommendations

310

country-tailored green growth recommendations, to almost 60 countries

CHAPTER 1

A FRAMEWORK TO ALIGN ECONOMIC AND ENVIRONMENTAL GOALS

This chapter presents an overview of the 2011 Green Growth Strategy to provide the background to this report. The Green Growth Strategy sets a framework for governments to foster economic growth and development, while ensuring that natural assets continue to provide the resources and environmental services vital to human well-being. The four principle elements of the strategy are presented including: aligning economic and environmental objectives; implementing policy frameworks to price pollution and promote efficient resource use and aligning sector-specific policies with green growth objectives; addressing green growth's social implications; and implementing mechanisms to evaluate and monitor progress.

The 2011 Green Growth Strategy provided important initial guidance to governments on driving growth while preserving natural capital. This chapter sets out its principal elements as background to the report.

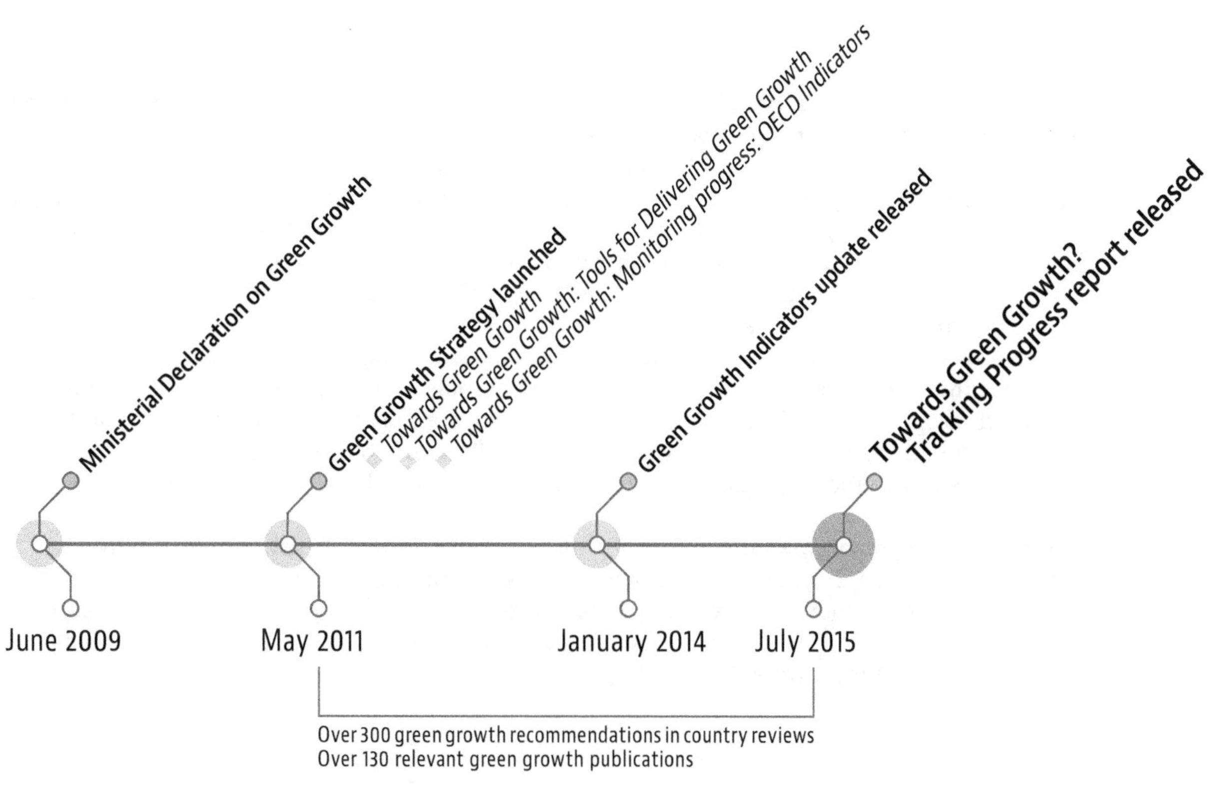

The 2011 Green Growth Strategy: "Green" and "growth" must go hand-in-hand. In 2009, OECD ministers agreed to strengthen efforts to pursue green growth as part of response measures to the financial crisis, recognising the dangers of a return to "business as usual" post-crisis.[1] They asked the OECD to develop a Green Growth Strategy to help the governments of OECD countries and partner economies alike achieve economic recovery along with environmentally and socially sustainable growth. The 2011 Green Growth Strategy responded to this mandate (OECD, 2011a, 2011b, 2011c, 2011d). It sets a framework for governments to foster economic growth and development, while ensuring that natural assets continue to provide the resources and environmental services vital to human well-being. Green growth is narrower in scope than the related concept of sustainable development. It focuses more squarely on driving progress at the interface of the economy and the environment by fostering innovation, investment and competition, thereby creating new sources of economic growth that are consistent with resilient and sustainable ecosystems (OECD, 2011a).

THE GREEN GROWTH STRATEGY

The need to reframe growth. Further economic opportunities are needed to improve the living standards of a growing global population. Yet risks to growth and development continue to rise as traditional growth models negatively affect the physical environment that ultimately underpins human well-being.

Water scarcity, worsening resource bottlenecks, greater pollution, climate change and biodiversity loss can undermine growth. Imbalances in natural systems raise the risk of more profound, abrupt and highly damaging environmental impacts that are not necessarily foreseeable on the basis of past experience. Climate change and biodiversity loss in particular represent systemic risks to growth, with greater risks to physical capital from more intense and frequent storms, droughts and floods, and risks to essential ecosystem services such as water purification, flood protection and carbon sequestration. The circumstances in each country are different, but as natural capital erodes and is replaced with increasingly costly and limited physical capital, possible resource bottlenecks may undermine gains from future economic activity and hinder growth.

Natural capital: A pillar for growth.

Mismanaging and undervaluing natural resources such as land and ecosystems can also impose substantial human and economic costs. For example, the estimated costs to society of outdoor air pollution, in terms of lives lost and ill health, were USD 1.7 trillion (US dollars) in 2010 in OECD countries alone (OECD, 2014), USD 1.3 trillion in China and USD 2.5 trillion in India. A narrow definition of economic growth, such as gross domestic product, does not account for these costs – hence the need for broader measures of prosperity that fully recognise the role of natural capital in economic growth and human well-being, as well as the limits and costs of existing production technology and consumer behaviour.

Opportunities can also arise from green growth through, for example, expanding markets for green technologies and services, improved market confidence from environmental policy clarity, and incentives for innovation and efficiency improvements. Economic opportunities can also result from newly created jobs, efficient management of natural resources and productivity gains (OECD, 2011a).

Four steps to green growth. The Green Growth Strategy sets a framework for governments to drive economic growth while preserving natural capital. It proposes four main steps: align economic and environmental objectives; implement policy frameworks to price pollution and promote efficient resource use; address green growth's social implications; and implement mechanisms to evaluate and monitor progress (Figure 1.1).

FIGURE 1.1. FOUR STEPS TO GREEN GROWTH: THE 2011 GREEN GROWTH STRATEGY

ALIGN GROWTH AND ENVIRONMENTAL OBJECTIVES

Gear core economic policies to mutually reinforce growth and conservation of natural capital.

- Link environmental objectives with economic reform policies.
- Anchor green growth in core economic ministries; drive cross-portfolio co-ordination.
- Address constraints to green investment and innovation.

Step 2

IMPLEMENT GREEN GROWTH POLICY FRAMEWORKS

Develop policy packages to price pollution and provide incentives for efficient resource use.

- Pricing instruments to drive broad-based, least cost action (tradable permit systems, taxes).
- Regulation to provide incentives for green growth (emissions performance standards, energy efficiency).
- Subsidies to promote green technologies, products and practices; fossil fuel subsidy reform.
- Information measures to guide consumer behaviour.

Gear sectoral policies for green growth.

- INVESTMENT AND FINANCE | INNOVATION
- TAXATION | TRADE AND FOREIGN DIRECT INVESTMENT
- ENERGY | TRANSPORT | AGRICULTURE
- WATER | BIODIVERSITY AND ECOSYSTEMS
- WASTE | CLIMATE CHANGE
- DEVELOPMENT | GREEN CITIES AND REGIONS
- FISHERIES

Step 3

ADDRESS THE SOCIAL IMPLICATIONS OF GREEN GROWTH

Address distributional impacts to facilitate reform and promote inclusiveness.

- Labour market and skills policies to transition workers across sectors.
- Compensation to address impacts on lower-income households.
- Multilateral coordination to address firm competitiveness concerns.

Step 4

MONITOR PROGRESS

Develop indicators to track progress.

- Transition to a low-carbon, resource efficient economy.
- Preservation of the natural asset base.
- Environmental quality of life.
- Economic opportunities and effective policy.

STEP 1: Align economic growth and environmental objectives

Embed environmental challenges at the heart of economic policy making. As environmental risks can undermine growth and human well-being, economic policies to promote growth and raise living standards must factor in these risks. This means aligning economic growth and environmental objectives in a consistent set of policy criteria and setting a longer time frame for making economic policy decisions.

There is no one-size-fits-all prescription, but all countries must marry economic and environmental priorities for green growth.

There is no one-size-fits-all prescription: countries' policy and institutional settings, development levels, resource endowments and environmental pressure points will differ. Nevertheless, green growth needs to be underpinned by a range of framework policies to reinforce jointly economic growth and natural capital conservation. Good economic policy lies at the heart of green growth because a flexible, dynamic economy will best spur the transition. Well-designed and executed core fiscal and regulatory settings for growth in areas such as tax and competition can help improve resource allocation. They can also decouple economic activity from natural capital depletion and open up new and greener sources of growth. The challenge is to align core economic principles in a logical and coherent long-term framework that takes full account of the value of natural capital as a criterion for growth, and focuses on cost-effective ways to relieve environmental pressures and avoid crossing critical thresholds.

As a first step, national governments should determine environmental priorities by diagnosing long-term conditions and risks, as well as the most cost-effective policy options and action areas (e.g. manage water scarcity, advance environment-related innovation) based on robust cost-benefit analysis. As a second step, they should link environmental objectives to economic reform priorities. Green growth strategies should target areas presenting clearly beneficial overlap between environmental and economic policies. They should investigate linkages between economic reform priorities and major constraints to green growth, e.g. improving infrastructure or the quality of innovation policies.

Integrating green growth objectives into broader economic policy making and development planning means that finance and economic ministries, as well as environment ministries, have a major role to play. Most countries will require new governance arrangements to help align economic and environmental policies, and overcome institutional inertia in policy making. Embedding green growth into core policy processes entails establishing leadership at the highest levels of government, driving co-operation between relevant ministries and government levels, building capacity, and including environmental issues in national development and poverty reduction planning.

Green growth strategies must consciously diagnose and address existing economic constraints or distortions inhibiting returns on green investment and innovation so as not to impede reform. This may involve, for example, reforming product-market regulations to enhance competition in network industries with heavy environmental impact (e.g. the electricity sector) or strong control over strategic environmental services (e.g. water). Removing institutional and regulatory barriers that protect incumbent firms and impose stringent requirements on new entrants can help generate new and greener economic activity.

STEP 2: Implement green growth policy frameworks

Design policies that put a price on pollution and provide incentives for efficient resource use. A number of policy tools are relevant in this regard.

- **Pricing instruments:** pricing instruments, e.g. tradable permit systems and taxes, drive broad-based action to reduce environmental damage at least cost and should be a central pillar of green growth policy (OECD, 2013a). They provide incentives for further efficiency gains, green investment and innovation. Importantly, increased or more effective use of environmentally related taxes can drive growth-oriented reform (by shifting the tax burden away from more distortive taxes, e.g. on corporate or personal income) and contribute to fiscal consolidation (i.e. by reducing government deficits and debt accumulation).

Beyond core policy tools, sectoral policy must be geared for green growth.

- **Regulation:** in some cases, regulation may be better suited than (or an important complement to) pricing instruments. Regulation represents an opportunity to promote green growth through initiatives such as emissions performance standards or measures targeting improved resource use (e.g. energy-efficiency standards). Depending on their design, regulatory instruments may be less cost-effective than direct pricing mechanisms, but can be important to advancing reform in countries where constituencies are strongly opposed to pricing reform and in areas that are not sufficiently responsive to price signals.

- **Subsidies:** policy makers commonly use subsidies to promote new and immature technologies and shift the balance of incentives towards more environmentally sound products and practices. Greening growth also means eliminating the subsidies for environmentally harmful resource use. A prominent example is support for fossil-fuel production and consumption: in 2013, support for fossil-fuel consumption, predominantly in developing and emerging economies, totalled around USD 548 billion – more than four times the amount spent on renewable energy (International Energy Agency [IEA], 2013). In OECD countries, support for fossil-fuel consumption and production ranged from USD 55 billion to USD 90 billion from 2005 to 2011 (OECD, 2013b). Fossil-fuel subsidies are only one example of subsidies that are harmful to the environment; many other areas (e.g. agriculture) also require consideration.

- **Guiding consumer behaviour:** information-based measures can strengthen consumer and business responsiveness to price signals by highlighting the negative environmental consequences of specific activities, the longer-term financial savings from using greener products and the availability of cleaner alternatives.

Align sector-specific policies with green growth objectives. Regulatory action will be required to gear existing sectoral and issue-specific policy towards supporting green growth, including by removing major barriers or distortions. When poorly aligned, sectoral policies (and core growth settings) can create unintended obstacles to reform (Box 1.1).

BOX 1.1 – ALIGNING POLICIES FOR THE TRANSITION TO A LOW-CARBON ECONOMY

The 2014 OECD Ministerial Council Meeting (MCM) mandated the OECD to examine how to improve policy alignment across different areas in order to enable a successful transition towards a sustainable low-carbon and climate-resilient economy, and to report back to the 2015 MCM. While emission-reduction policies are essential, core climate policies necessarily involve numerous other areas: the required policy instruments and economic signals operate on top of existing frameworks, intersect with other policy goals and interact with their dedicated instruments. This may lead to frictions and unintended consequences, or policy working at cross-purposes.

The "Aligning Policies for the Transition to a Low-carbon Economy" project identifies policy misalignments that hamper low-carbon policies' effectiveness and provides guidance on resolving them. It seeks to extend climate policy discussions to ministers and parts of government not typically involved in them, recognising that they can play a significant role in delivering emission reductions at least cost.

STEP 3: Address the social implications of green growth

Addressing the distributional consequences of policies on current generations is important for reform. Labour market, household and firm impacts are all relevant.

Transitional policies can minimise the negative short-term labour market consequences of shifting towards green growth. Green growth is unlikely to generate a windfall gain in jobs or a sharp increase in labour market churn, even though it will create additional jobs in flourishing sectors such as renewable energy. As green growth takes hold, polluting industries will need to fundamentally change technologies or shed jobs. As for workers, an increasing number will need to acquire new skills to perform in environmentally friendly jobs, whether newly created or re-engineered. Labour market and skill policies are essential in order to minimise skill bottlenecks, prevent a rise in structural unemployment and help workers move from contracting to expanding sectors. The potentially large income effects of these changes for some workers also raise concerns over the equitable distribution of gains and losses.

Potential labour market, household and firm impacts are all relevant for reform.

Address regressive effects of reform. Some green growth measures may have a disproportionate impact on poorer households. This may require, at least as a transitional measure, targeted compensation programmes that go beyond the compensation already offered by a well-functioning tax and welfare system. Such measures are likely to play a prominent role in emerging and developing markets in particular, where social safety nets are less developed and some populations may be more vulnerable to the transitional costs associated with green growth.

Assess business concerns over potential competitiveness impacts. Firms may assert that green growth causes cost increases that diminish their competitiveness (including against overseas competitors subjected to less stringent environmental standards) or undermine return on investment. Assessing the extent of any unintended losses – which are traditionally associated with climate mitigation measures – requires understanding how the economy as a whole will likely adjust to new environmental regulation. Some mechanisms, e.g. multilateral policy co-ordination, may be warranted to address potential "pollution haven" effects, whereby foreign markets pick up local industries' lost production.[2]

STEP 4: Implement mechanisms to evaluate and monitor green growth progress

The Green Growth Strategy proposes 26 indicators to track progress – including at the international level – across four areas (Figure 1.2). First, the transition to a low-carbon, resource-efficient economy – how productive are environmental assets and natural resources? Second, the natural asset base – a declining asset base represents a risk to growth. Third, environmental quality of life – what are the environment's direct impacts on human well-being? Fourth, economic opportunities and effective policy – how well is policy delivering on green growth and its associated economic opportunities? These indicators aim to help determine policy's effectiveness in delivering green growth. Indicators that reflect the socio-economic characteristics of growth (e.g. economic growth, productivity and competitiveness; and labour markets, education and income) can complete the picture, by helping to track the effect of green growth policies on growth and establish links to social objectives such as poverty reduction, social equity and inclusion.[3]

FIGURE 1.2 – TWENTY-SIX GREEN GROWTH INDICATORS

TRANSITION TO A RESOURCE-EFFICIENT, LOW-CARBON ECONOMY

How efficient is the use of environmental resources and services?

Carbon productivity

Energy productivity
- Energy Productivity GDP per unit of TPES
- Energy intensity by sector
- Share of renewable energy sources

Resource productivity
- Demand-based material productivity
- Waste generation intensity/recovery ratios
- Nutrient flows and balances

Water productivity

Environmentally adjusted, whole-economy (multi-factor) productivity

NATURAL ASSET BASE

Are environmental and economic resources being preserved, to support future growth?

Natural resource index

Freshwater

Forests

Fish

Minerals

Land

Soil

Wildlife

ENVIRONMENTAL QUALITY OF LIFE

How are environment conditions impacting on human well-being? What kind of access does the public have to environmental services and amenities?

Environmentally induced health problems and related costs

Exposure to natural or industrial risks and related economic losses

Access to sewage treatment and drinking water
- Population connected to sewage treatment
- Population with sustainable access to safe drinking water

ECONOMIC OPPORTUNITIES AND EFFECTIVE POLICY

How effective is current green growth policy? Are the economic opportunities associated with the transition being seized?

R&D expenditure of importance to green growth

Patents of importance to green growth

Environment-related innovation in all sectors

Production of environmental goods and services

International financial flows of importance to green growth

Environmentally related taxation

Energy pricing

Water pricing and cost recovery

Regulations and management approaches

Training and skill development

The 2011 proposal for further work on green growth. The Green Growth Strategy package mapped a longer-term work agenda to support country implementation across three main areas. First, it proposed mainstreaming green growth analysis into OECD country surveillance exercises, thereby tailoring advice to the national level and providing targeted guidance for progress. Second, it proposed undertaking further work on green growth indicators to meet the challenge of matching the proposed OECD indicator framework with available internationally comparable data and improve the ability to track the transition at the country level. Finally, it proposed carrying out sectoral and issue-specific studies to provide more concrete insights into greening growth across relevant areas, including agriculture, energy, water, biodiversity and development co-operation. The proposal also flagged the need for further analysis on the costs and benefits of various policy instruments, as well as the possibility of developing a cross-country analytical tool to identify country-specific policy priorities. The analysis in this report is informed by work undertaken across these areas since 2011.

CHAPTER REFERENCES

IEA (2013), *World Energy Outlook 2013,* IEA, Paris. http://dx.doi.org/10.1787/weo-2013-en.

OECD (2014), *The Cost of Air Pollution: Health Impacts of Road Transport,* OECD Publishing, Paris, http://dx.doi.org/10.1787/9789264210448-en.

OECD (2013a), *Effective Carbon Prices,* OECD Publishing, Paris, http://dx.doi.org/10.1787/9789264196964-en.

OECD (2013b), *Inventory of Estimated Budgetary Support and Tax Expenditures for Fossil Fuels 2013,* OECD Publishing, Paris, http://dx.doi.org/10.1787/9789264187610-en.

OECD (2011a), *Towards Green Growth,* OECD Green Growth Studies, OECD Publishing, Paris, http://dx.doi.org/10.1787/9789264111318-en.

OECD (2011b), "Towards Green Growth: A Summary for Policy Makers", brochure prepared the OECD Meeting of the Council at Ministerial Level, 25-26 May, 2011, OECD, Paris, www.oecd.org/greengrowth/48012345.pdf.

OECD (2011c), "Tools for Delivering on Green Growth", prepared for the OECD Meeting of the Council at Ministerial Level, 25-26 May, 2011, OECD, Paris, www.oecd.org/greengrowth/48012326.pdf.

OECD (2011d), *Towards Green Growth: Monitoring Progress: OECD Indicators,* OECD Green Growth Studies, OECD Publishing, Paris, http://dx.doi.org/10.1787/9789264111356-en.

1 "Declaration on Green Growth", adopted at the OECD Council Meeting at Ministerial level on 25 June 2009: www.oecd.org/officialdocuments/publicdisplaydocumentpdf/?doclanguage=en&cote=C/MIN(2009)5/ADD1/FINAL.

2 Recent work suggests that industry largely overstates the competitiveness impacts of environmental reform: see Chapter 4.

3 The OECD Green Growth Indicator framework is reflected in joint work by the OECD, the Global Green Growth Institute, the United Nations Environment Programme and the World Bank as part of the Green Growth Knowledge Platform's programme on green growth measurement and indicators (see *Moving Towards a Common Approach on Green Growth Indicators,* www.greengrowthknowledge.org/resource/moving-towards-common-approach-green-growth-indicators).

CHAPTER 2

COUNTRY EFFORTS TO IMPLEMENT **GREEN GROWTH**

This chapter provides a preliminary assessment of the major challenges to implementing green growth policy frameworks at the national level. The challenges are derived from the green growth policy recommendations contained in the country surveillance work that the OECD has completed since the release of the 2011 Green Growth Strategy *(Economic Surveys, Environmental Policy Reviews, Investment Policy Reviews and Reviews of Innovation Policy).* The most common green growth challenges relate to: implementing market instruments to price pollution and natural-resource use; orienting tax systems to advance green growth; designing environmentally relevant subsidies; and gearing sectoral policy towards green growth. The challenges are not exhaustive, but provide useful lessons for governments on how to accelerate and improve green growth policy implementation, and allow for the identification of a number of broader observations on country experience to date.

Countries are taking steps to implement policy frameworks for green growth, but more concerted efforts are needed to truly align economic and environmental priorities. Lessons from common challenges can help governments accelerate progress.

Four years after the launch of the Green Growth Strategy, governments have taken steps towards green growth. Most countries have implemented some measures to begin pricing pollution and provide incentives for efficient resource use, such as pricing instruments, regulatory measures and subsidies.[1] Around one-third of OECD countries and a number of OECD partner economies have adapted, or are adapting, the Green Growth Strategy's indicator framework to help evaluate and monitor progress towards national green growth objectives (OECD, 2014a).

Much more concerted efforts are needed to meaningfully align economic and environmental priorities. To drive green growth, governments must embed environmental challenges at the heart of economic policy making, by linking environmental and economic reform priorities in a consistent set of objectives. Finance and economic ministries have a major role to play. A number of countries have taken relevant measures, including developing green growth strategies and inter-ministry committees co-ordinating elements of green growth policy. Yet no country has comprehensively linked environmental and economic reform priorities. Measurability also remains a challenge, as many countries lack data over sufficient time periods to enable effective assessment of policies.

Common challenges in implementing green growth demonstrate broad scope for reform.

Drawing lessons from common experience. Since 2011, the Green Growth Strategy has been tailored to take into account country-specific circumstances. The country surveillance undertaken by the OECD enables a preliminary assessment of major challenges to implementing green growth policy frameworks at the national level. This chapter examines the eight most common challenges addressed by green growth policy recommendations in *OECD Economic Surveys, Environmental Policy Reviews, Investment Policy Reviews and Reviews of Innovation Policy* (Figure 2.1).[2] The challenges relate to implementing market instruments to price pollution and natural-resource use; orienting tax systems to advance green growth; designing environmentally relevant subsidies; and gearing sectoral policy towards green growth.

The challenges addressed in this chapter are not exhaustive; rather, they highlight where broad scope exists to heighten the ambition and effectiveness of green growth policy across countries. Green growth policy design and mainstreaming are ongoing, the range of relevant issues is broad and the challenges countries face are different (Table 2.1). The eight most common challenges addressed in this chapter will not necessarily apply to all countries. Rather, they demonstrate where some of the main opportunities to accelerate and improve green growth policy implementation lie across countries. Other challenges remain relevant, depending on the country in question.

FIGURE 2.1 - EIGHT MOST COMMON GREEN GROWTH CHALLENGES ADDRESSED IN OECD COUNTRY SURVEILLANCE

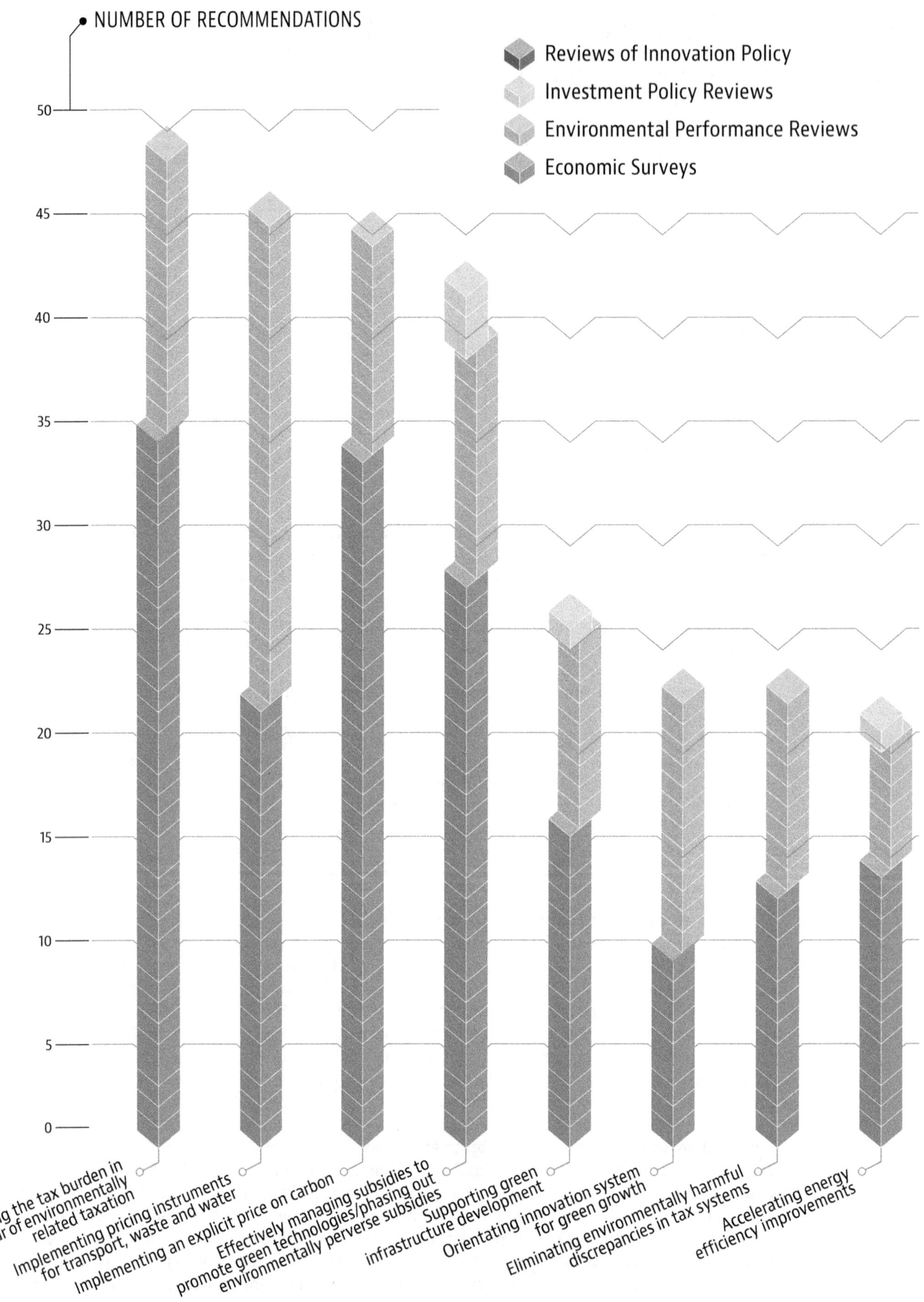

TABLE 2.1 – COUNTRY-SPECIFIC GREEN GROWTH CHALLENGES

Challenge No. 1: Establishing an explicit price on greenhouse gas emissions through taxation or tradable permit systems

Putting an explicit price on emissions. To transition to a green economy, governments need to send consistent market signals that the cost of carbon dioxide (CO_2) and other greenhouse gas emissions will gradually increase – otherwise companies will have little incentive to shift away from fossil fuels. Explicit carbon-pricing mechanisms that put a price on each tonne of carbon emitted are generally the most cost-effective means of creating strong economic incentives to reduce carbon emissions (OECD, 2013a). They minimise the cost of achieving mitigation targets by driving broad action, while providing incentives for innovation and investment in low-carbon technologies; they can also serve as a valuable source of government revenue, which can be used to decrease other, more distortive, taxes. Two explicit carbon-pricing mechanisms exist. The first are emissions trading systems, which establish an overall cap on the total level of greenhouse gas emissions and enable auctioning or allocating allowances. Liable entities can then redeem allowances for emitted CO_2, or trade unused allowances. The second mechanism is through direct carbon taxes, which establish a price per tonne directly linked to CO_2 emissions levels.

Carbon pricing is a cost effective way to reduce emissions, but faces political challenges.

Carbon pricing is expanding in developed, emerging and developing countries, but the scope for further uptake is great. An estimated 40 national and 20 subnational jurisdictions have implemented, or are considering implementing, an explicit price on carbon covering approximately 6 gigatonnes of carbon equivalent, or covering about 12% of annual global greenhouse gas emissions (World Bank, 2014). In some countries, the proportion of emissions covered is greater. While these measures are significant in representing concrete steps in the right direction, the carbon prices that have been established to date have generally been low and insufficient to spur technological change or significantly alter consumer behaviour. China and the United States, the world's two largest emitters, have carbon systems operating at the subnational level. On 12 November 2014, they jointly announced a plan to strengthen bilateral and multilateral co-operation on climate change, with the aim of adopting an ambitious climate agreement at the 2015 United Nations Climate Change Conference (COP21). The countries made national-level pledges: China promised to peak carbon emissions by 2030 and increase the share of non-fossil fuels in primary energy consumption to around 20% by 2030, while the United States vowed to achieve economy-wide emissions reductions of 26-28% below 2005 levels by 2025.[3] If carbon pricing became an element of these pledges, the coverage of global greenhouse gas emissions would increase significantly.

Carbon pricing is an indispensable policy tool, but political opposition is a fundamental challenge. Case studies of initiatives in jurisdictions such as Ireland (Convery, Dunne and Joyce, 2013) and the Canadian province of British Columbia (Harrison, 2013) demonstrate that leadership, consultation, incremental implementation and transparent analysis can contribute to successfully introducing pricing mechanisms. In the case of carbon taxes, recycling tax revenues back to consumers – e.g. by reducing income or business taxes and increasing budgetary allocations for social services – can help ease resistance to implementation. Nevertheless, carbon pricing remains politically challenging and is struggling to gain momentum in many parts of the world. Australia, for example, repealed its carbon-pricing legislation in 2014 and may now go without a core market mechanism for reducing greenhouse gas emissions in the indefinite future (OECD, 2014b). Once implemented, governments can also find it politically challenging to ensure that pricing mechanisms are sufficiently aggressive to reduce emissions (i.e. by increasing prices or significantly restricting the supply of permits in trading systems). This is particularly the case given many countries are yet to implement pricing measures, a fact which tends to heighten opposition from industry due to concerns over possible competitiveness impacts.

Addressing the social implications of carbon pricing is important to reform. Facilitating reform and ensuring equitable outcomes requires paying closer attention to its potential social impacts. Regressive impacts should be addressed through complementary measures that are clearly communicated – along with the motivation for change – to affected households and businesses. The paradox of carbon pricing lies in that despite its importance as a policy tool and the clear political challenges associated with reform, policy makers do not pay sufficient attention to its impact on the poor. It is telling that while carbon pricing represents the third most common green growth-relevant recommendation in OECD country reviews – addressed in 44 of 113 reports reviewed since 2011 (Figure 2.1) – its potential distributional impacts are among the least-referenced issues (Chapter 4): only 12 reviews discuss household impacts and 19 reference labour market impacts, for example. Yet we know that the distributional consequences of imposing a carbon tax in countries such as France have played a major part in undermining or delaying them. Ex post evaluation of the competitiveness impacts of environmental measures is one tool to assess potential detrimental effects of carbon pricing on firm output or employment, but it is currently underutilised (Arlinghaus, 2015).

Challenge No. 2: Using pricing instruments to change behaviour with respect to water, waste and transport

Pricing mechanisms can of course be used beyond carbon pricing to influence consumer, producer and investor behaviour in order to reduce pollution and other external costs, address inefficiencies and reflect resource scarcity. Pricing instruments in the combined water, waste and transport areas feature in 45 reviews, making them the second most common focus area for green growth (Figure 2.1).

Sustainable financing to manage water resources, including through water tariffs and water prices, remains a challenge. Ensuring the environmental sustainability of water ecosystems, reducing flood and drought impacts, and maximising access to water supply and sanitation requires sustainable financing. Despite an already significant asset base, the cost of modernising and upgrading water systems in OECD countries is estimated at 0.4-1.2% of gross domestic product (GDP) a year for the next 20 years (OECD, 2012a). Developing countries need an estimated USD 18 billion (US dollars) a year to increase the level of population with access to an improved water supply, on top of the approximate USD 54 billion needed to maintain existing services. Sustainable financing of the water sector is essential, but remains challenging for many governments. Aligning incentives through tariffs and water prices, as well as promoting private financing and sound governance, are important means to this end.

0.4-1.2% of GDP, annual cost of modernising water systems in OECD countries, making sustainable financing essential.

Several countries have made efforts to reform water-financing mechanisms, e.g. by introducing tariffs, user charges, pollution charges, cost recovery instruments and water markets (OECD, 2012a).OECD countries are making efforts to increase cost recovery, and prices in developing countries also appear to be rising. While these measures help cover the costs associated with providing water service and managing sustainable supply and demand, much more remains to be done. OECD advice to countries such as Australia, Austria, Belgium, Colombia, Israel, Italy, Mexico, New Zealand, South Africa and Spain (OECD, 2012b, 2013b, 2011a, 2011b, 2013c, 2013d, 2013e, 2013f, 2014c; OECD/ECLAC, 2014) continues to encourage using pricing mechanisms to support the management and sustainable financing of water resources.

Pricing instruments form an important part of the policy toolset needed to drive resource efficiency, reduce waste and move towards a circular economy. OECD countries are accelerating efforts to transition to a more resource-efficient economy, i.e. an economy that maximises the quantity of output produced with a given input of natural resources and minimises environmental impacts per unit of output produced. They are showing signs of decoupling material consumption from economic growth: GDP per material input has increased by about 30% since 2000. The amount of municipal waste – around 10% of total waste – has decreased by almost 4% over the past decade; meanwhile, the amount of material and energy recovery from waste has grown, thanks to efforts to treat waste as a resource. Recycling rates are increasing (by up to 80% in some cases) for important materials such as glass, steel, aluminium, paper and plastics (OECD, 2015a). In Germany, for example, material consumption has decreased at the same time as economic growth has increased, both before and after the economic crisis. More sustainable waste management has played its part: the country has used effective pricing (among other policy measures) to reduce municipal waste, improve waste recovery and reduce landfill (OECD, 2012c).

Despite progress in OECD countries, global material consumption continues to increase, in line with world GDP, as a result of higher material use in emerging economies. Further efforts are required to decouple GDP and material consumption, including in OECD countries, where per capita consumption stands at about 60% above the world average.

The use of economic instruments to encourage more sustainable materials management – including landfill taxes and incineration taxes – is expanding. However, the high number of economic actors and sectors implicated in promoting resource productivity, combined with the lack of comprehensive data, make implementation difficult (OECD, 2014d). Further work is needed to advance pricing instruments as part of a mix of policy tools addressing different stages of the resource life cycle (e.g. deposit refunds, upstream combined taxes and subsidies, and take-back requirements).

In addition to motor vehicle taxation, distance-based charging and congestion charging have an important role to play in reducing environmental and other externalities associated with road transport. The transport sector accounts for around 18% of primary energy use globally and 20% of associated CO_2 emissions (International Energy Agency [IEA], 2014a). Road vehicles are responsible for the largest share – just under 40% of global energy consumption – in the sector. They are also to blame for a high proportion of outdoor air pollution and the resulting costs to society: initial estimates suggest that they account for about half of the approximately USD 1.7 trillion in costs associated with the health impacts of outdoor air pollution in OECD countries (OECD, 2014e). Road transport also represents a large proportion of the USD 1.4 trillion in health costs associated with air pollution in China and USD 0.5 trillion in associated health costs in India.[4] In addition to these environmental and social costs, the economic costs associated with road-traffic congestion can be significant. In Belgium, time lost in traffic jams and behavioural changes resulting from congestion – such as lower labour mobility – are estimated to cost around 1-2% of GDP (OECD, 2013g). The volume of road-vehicle passenger transport is projected to rise by 60% between 2010 and 2050 in OECD countries and to increase 4 or 5 times over outside the OECD, exacerbating associated externalities (OECD/ITF, 2013).

Pricing mechanisms help address externalities associated with road transport.

Strong new policies, including pricing mechanisms, are required to address the externalities associated with road transport. In almost all countries, motor vehicle fuels are among the most heavily taxed energy products, but road pricing mechanisms – e.g. tolls or congestion charges – also have an important role to play in encouraging a shift to cleaner modes of transport (e.g. walking, cycling and public transportation [Ang and Marchal, 2013]). While user charges are universally accepted as part of public transportation, social acceptance of road pricing to reflect at least some proportion of environmental, social and economic costs is more difficult to achieve (Banister, Crist and Perkins, 2015). Around one-sixth of OECD country reviews since 2011 provide advice on tackling this issue (Figure 2.1). Emphasising non-climate-related policy benefits can be an effective way of building local support for measures such as congestion charges and land value capture tools (Ang and Marchal, 2013).

Challenge No. 3: Shifting the tax burden in favour of environmentally related taxation

Environmentally related taxation is a cost-effective but underutilised tool to achieve environmental objectives. Environmentally related taxation ensures market prices reflect some proportion of the environmental costs associated with economic activity. By adjusting relative prices, it helps shift producer and consumer behaviour towards more environmentally beneficial activities and products. Empirical evidence supports the traditional textbook claim that environmentally related taxation is a cost-effective means of achieving environmental objectives (OECD, 2013a).

Almost all OECD countries, and many non-OECD countries, now use environmentally related taxes (Greene and Braathen, 2014). Yet the revenue raised through them, expressed as a percentage of GDP, remains limited in many countries. In OECD countries, revenue from environmentally related taxes represents on average 2% of GDP.[5] This share has remained stagnant over the past 15 years, in part because rising international fuel prices have reduced demand – and hence tax revenue – from motor fuels.

Revenue raised from environmentally related taxation remains limited in many countries.

The share of environmentally related taxes as a percentage of GDP is higher (over 3.5% of GDP) in Slovenia, Denmark, Turkey and the Netherlands (Greene and Braathen, 2014). This suggests scope for further taxation in most other countries. Shifting part of the tax burden towards environmentally related taxation can also drive growth-oriented reform, by helping to reduce other more distortive taxes, e.g. on labour. New taxes can also help reduce government deficits and debt accumulation, and thus represent an attractive alternative to public expenditure cuts or higher taxes on labour or business income. OECD country surveillance reports' heavy focus on this issue – it features in 49 reports, ranking highest on the list of issues discussed – demonstrates the scope for improvement across countries (Figure 2.1).

Challenge No. 4: Eliminating environmentally harmful discrepancies in tax systems

Gearing tax systems towards supporting green growth means ensuring that taxation policy is coherent from an environmental perspective – whether or not it specifically targets environmental objectives – in addition to relying more on environmentally related taxation.

The structure and level of taxes on energy use are not coherent in many OECD countries, where 72% of all environmentally related tax revenue derives from taxes on energy products, including motor vehicle fuels (Harding, 2014a). Given the environmental and social costs (e.g. climate change, local air pollution, resource depletion, vulnerability to supply shocks) associated with using fossil fuels in particular, taxing energy use is vital to help ensure that energy prices and use better reflect associated costs. Yet recent work shows inconsistencies – with no obvious rationale – in the taxation of different forms, uses and users of energy in many OECD countries when assessed against environmental and other social costs (OECD, 2013h). These variations result in uneven price signals and suggest untapped low-cost opportunities for reform to ensure, where possible, that tax rates reflect the external costs associated with different forms of energy and energy use.[6] A common example is the difference between tax rates on diesel and gasoline for road use.

33 of 34 OECD countries tax diesel at lower rates than gasoline, despite greater environmental and social externalities.

Eliminating the difference in the tax treatment of gasoline and diesel for road use – i.e. addressing the "diesel differential" – is important. A full 33 out of 34 OECD countries tax diesel fuel at lower rates than gasoline, both in terms of energy and carbon content; the United States is the exception (Harding, 2014). This difference is not justifiable from an environmental perspective. As compared to gasoline, per litre diesel use is associated with higher levels of harmful local air pollutants, e.g. nitrogen oxide, sulphur dioxide and particulate matter; CO_2 emissions per litre of diesel are higher as well. This implies that the level of tax for a litre of diesel should be higher than for a litre of gasoline to reflect relative environmental costs. Diesel vehicles are also often more fuel-efficient and tend to travel farther per litre of fuel than gasoline vehicles, meaning that social costs such as congestion, noise, accidents and infrastructure wear are also higher on a per litre basis than for gasoline. This, too, justifies higher taxes on diesel than on gasoline, unless better instruments to account for driving-related external costs become much more widespread than they currently are.

The difference in tax rates on gasoline and diesel has sometimes been motivated by the fact that diesel-fuelled vehicles are more fuel-efficient (although this will tend to influence consumer decisions in favour of diesel, even in the absence of taxes) or that diesel is traditionally used in commercial transport. The different tax rate may also result from the incremental design and introduction of taxes on different energy products. However, as diesel produces greater negative environmental and social impacts than gasoline, its preferential tax treatment should be eliminated. Governments may wish to raise diesel tax rates gradually to help mitigate industry or household impacts (i.e. on commercial transport costs and corresponding price effects on economy-wide production costs or consumer-good price levels). More targeted forms of assistance, such as recycling the revenue from tax increases through direct transfers or tax rebates, may be more appropriate than other measures – e.g. exemptions – to avoid adverse environmental signals. signals (Harding, 2014a).

The European Commission has proposed revising its Energy Tax Directive to increase its minimum tax rate on diesel to EUR 0.39 per litre, higher than the tax on gasoline (EUR 0.36 per litre) (European Commission, 2011), but the differential remains in place in Europe and beyond.

The preferential tax treatment of company cars needs to be eliminated. Green growth-relevant tax policy goes beyond environmentally related taxation. For example, all OECD countries tax the use of company cars for personal purposes more favourably than they do wage income – significantly so in most cases (Harding, 2014b). At least two-thirds of OECD countries capture no more than 50% of the benefit to employees as a taxable benefit relative to a counter-factual benchmark of neutral tax treatment. In 2012, this represented an untaxed amount of approximately EUR 26.8 billion, reflecting that company cars represent a substantial proportion of the car fleet in many OECD countries.[7] Only two countries, Canada and Norway, capture more than 90% of the total counter-factual benchmark. The weighted average annual subsidy across countries is EUR 1 600 – large enough to suggest behavioural consequences.

EUR 116 billion, annual social costs attributable to under-taxation of company cars in OECD countries.

Thus, the current tax treatment of company cars is both fiscally and environmentally significant. And yet tax settings on company-car use can influence distances travelled, favour certain modes of (more polluting) transport and influence decisions on both housing location and vehicle choice, as well as contribute to traffic congestion, accidents, noise and other social costs. Most OECD countries do not tie their taxable benefits to the distance driven – which is one of the main factors of the discrepancy between actual and neutral tax settings (Roy, 2014). The countries that do so apply fixed per kilometre rates that fail to capture the benefit of additional fuel consumed by less-efficient vehicles. Only 20% of the distance component is captured as a taxable benefit compared to a tax-neutral scenario, which is likely to result in a disproportionally large increase in total distance driven and related environmental pressures.

Germany actually provides additional income tax deductions based on distances driven, resulting in an estimated 2 million tonnes of CO_2 emissions a year in 2015 and 2.6 million tonnes a year by 2030 (OECD, 2012c).

Overall social costs attributable to under-taxation of company cars across OECD countries – including additional congestion costs, local costs from air pollution costs and traffic accidents – are estimated at around EUR 116 billion a year – considerably more than the associated fiscal costs of EUR 26.8 billion a year in total tax revenue lost. Moreover, preferential tax treatment of company cars is regressive and favours higher income earners, providing considerable motivation to eliminate the favourable tax treatment of company cars across countries.

Challenge No. 5: Managing subsidies to promote green technologies and phasing out environmentally perverse subsidies

Subsidies, like pricing and environmentally related taxes, provide market signals that can influence producer and consumer behaviour. If well designed and targeted, they can help weight incentives in favour of more environmentally sound activities and products, address market failures, and drive green innovation and investment (Greene and Braathen, 2014). Conversely, support for environmentally harmful consumption or production, such as that associated with fossil fuels – unhelpfully still

USD 640 billion, annual government spending on environmentally harmful support for fossil fuels.

prevalent and substantial in both OECD countries and partner economies – works against environmental objectives. Eliminating such support should be a high policy priority to advance the green growth agenda.

Ensuring that subsidies – such as feed-in-tariffs that aim to promote green technologies and practices – effectively advance change is an ongoing challenge. Governments spent an estimated USD 121 billion on renewable-energy subsidies worldwide in 2013 (IEA, 2014b). When using green subsidies, governments must remain flexible enough to ensure affordable and efficient support schemes that react to reductions in technology costs, while ensuring market signals are sufficiently clear and stable to drive change. Mixed messages, "stop-and-go" policy making and retroactive policy changes can seriously weaken market signals, as recently happened in the renewables sector. In the United States, only 1 gigawatt of new wind power capacity was installed in 2013 – a fraction of the 13 gigawatts installed in 2012 – following the anticipated expiration of a tax credit on renewable electricity production at the end of 2012 (IEA, 2014b); the credit was subsequently extended in late 2012. Targeting, finding or redirecting limited public funds can also prove challenging, as can meeting administrative capacity and information requirements. OECD policy advice to China, France, Germany, Ireland, Israel, Japan, Jordan and Portugal, as well as other countries across the European Union, bears out these challenges (OECD, 2013i, 2013j, 2012c, 2011c, 2011b, 2013k, 2013l, 2012d, 2014f).

It is estimated that governments currently spend over USD 640 billion a year on environmentally harmful support for fossil fuels. This support directly counteracts green growth efforts, by acting as a negative price on carbon and holding back investment in cleaner energy technologies. In 2009, Group of Twenty (G20) leaders made a commitment to "rationalise and phase out over the medium term inefficient fossil-fuel subsidies that encourage wasteful consumption" and called on the rest of the world to do the same. Much work remains to be done. OECD countries continue to support the production of fossil fuels in many ways – e.g. through market intervention that affects costs or prices; direct transfers; risk assumption; preferential tax treatment; and undercharging for use of government-supplied goods or assets – effectively shoring up the already significant advantage of incumbent technologies and making it harder for new, cleaner technologies to compete for market share. They also support energy consumption, e.g. through price controls regulating the cost of energy to consumers; direct transfers; consumer rebates on purchases of energy products; and tax relief.

The OECD *Inventory of Estimated Budgetary Support and Tax Expenditures for Fossil Fuels* (OECD, 2013m) identifies over 550 measures supporting the use or production of fossil fuels in OECD countries, broken down by country.[8] The total estimated value of these measures ranged from USD 55-90 billion a year between 2005 and 2011; around two-thirds of the measures target petroleum, with the remainder split between coal and natural gas.

The level of support in emerging and developing countries – an estimated USD 550 billion in 2013 in consumption support alone – is even greater (IEA, 2014c). Not only do these subsidies for fossil-fuel consumption absorb substantial public resources that could be put to better use elsewhere, they largely benefit the wealthy, even though governments often justify them on the grounds of alleviating energy poverty. In Indonesia, for example, fossil-fuel subsidy expenditure reached an estimated 24% of GDP in 2013 (OECD, 2015b); in 2009, 40% of the country's subsidies went to the richest 10% of households, and only 1% to the poorest 10% of households. The Indonesian government continues to pursue reform, however. At the beginning of 2015, it grasped the opportunity offered by falling world oil prices to scrap its existing petrol and diesel price-setting regime. Prices are now linked to world prices, although diesel retains a fixed subsidy of IDR 1 000 (rupiahs) (USD 0.08). In India, it is estimated that the implicit subsidy on oil is seven times higher for the richest 10% of households than the poorest 10% (OECD, 2014g) and yet reform often faces public resistance. OECD provides ongoing advice on fossil-fuel subsidy reform, including how to better target measures to address energy poverty, e.g. through direct transfers.

Challenge No. 6: Supporting the development of green infrastructure

Infrastructure choices made today have significant long-term implications for the environment. Greening infrastructure is required to avoid technology lock-in over the long term. For example, a coal-fired power station that comes on line today is likely to last 50-60 years, locking in local impacts from air pollution and greenhouse gas emissions for decades to come unless its economic life is prematurely curtailed (Corfee-Morlot et al., 2012). In the energy sector, the IEA estimates that around 80% of possible cumulative emissions to 2035 under an energy scenario consistent with international climate goals are already accounted for, based on the infrastructure currently in place and under construction (IEA, 2012). This leaves very little room for additional polluting facilities, unless governments are prepared to enforce premature infrastructure retirement or leave capacity idle in time. If international climate mitigation targets are to be met, 80% of power plant investments will need to be in low-carbon technologies after 2020, and 90% after 2025 (IEA, 2014a).

80% of possible energy-sector cumulative emissions to 2035 in a low-carbon scenario are accounted for by existing or planned energy infrastructure.

The green investment challenge may be more about channelling investment towards the right kind of infrastructure than unlocking significant amounts of additional capital (OECD, 2013n). Around USD 2 trillion is invested annually in transport,[9] energy and water infrastructure, representing around 4% of global GDP. An additional USD 1.2 trillion is required every year to maintain current levels of infrastructure capacity and service in these sectors, as well as support development and growth to 2030. This figure does not take into account environmental constraints (Kaminker et al., 2013). A shift to "green" investment across these sectors could require additional spending. The "New Climate Economy" report estimates that the transition to a low-carbon economy, for example, would add a 5% incremental cost, as low-carbon infrastructure is often more capital-intensive than fossil-fuel assets (New Climate Economy, 2014). Yet green infrastructure investment also has the potential to drive savings if systematic investment in the right kind of infrastructure enables capturing system-wide efficiency gains. Studies suggest net savings in the order of USD 450 billion, or a 14% reduction in overall cost resulting from changes such as the better use of electricity grids through smart grid deployment (Kennedy and Corfee-Morlot, 2013). The IEA estimates that USD 44 trillion in additional investment to decarbonise the energy system, in line with international climate goals, would yield fuel savings of USD 71 trillion by 2050 (IEA, 2014a).

The investment policy environment is vital to directing private investment towards "clean" infrastructure. Given the scale of investment needed and the current strains on public finances, engaging private-sector investment will be essential. However, governments cannot assume that capital will simply flow in the quantities and timeframe required to achieve the green transition on its own; public support stemming from clear, long-term and stable policy signals is an essential part of the business case for green investment (Kaminker et al., 2013). Policy makers need to address a range of government and market failures, as well as other investment barriers, which collectively favour investing in fossil fuel-intensive activities over investing in clean infrastructure. In addition to core green growth policy settings (e.g. pricing mechanisms, regulation), this means examining existing rules, regulations and policies that may restrict green infrastructure investment; creating investment vehicles that generate the risk-return ratios required by investors (OECD, 2015c); promoting collaborative dialogue among investors and across different levels of government; and compiling and sharing the data needed for investors to evaluate the risks and performance of green infrastructure investments (Kaminker et al., 2013). Governments also need to pay attention to barriers to international investment (e.g. local content requirements) that may hinder green infrastructure investment (Bahar, Egeland and Steenblik, 2013; OECD, forthcoming a).

Institutional investors are a particularly promising source of finance, but currently invest little in green and non-green infrastructure projects alike; further policy measures are required to address the specific challenges they face. In 2013, institutional investors in OECD countries (e.g. insurance companies, investment funds, pension funds, public pension reserve funds, foundations and endowments) held USD 93 trillion worth of assets (OECD, 2015c). Traditional sources of green infrastructure investments, such as governments and banks, face increasing constraints due to structural obstacles, deleveraging and impending financial regulations. Institutional investors could play a key role in financing the transition in this context. In emerging and developing countries, sovereign wealth funds are key sources of capital, thanks to their USD 7 trillion in assets as of January 2015 (Sovereign Wealth Fund Institute, 2015). Yet institutional investors' allocations to green infrastructure remain low: large pension funds allocated only 1% of their assets directly to infrastructure projects of all types in 2013 – of which only an estimated 3% went to green infrastructure investment (OECD, 2014h). Beyond the measures mentioned above, potential additional measures to catalyse further investment include establishing a national infrastructure strategy and road map, facilitating the development and application of risk mitigants, reducing the transaction costs associated with investing in sustainable energy and establishing a dedicated green investment bank.

Institutional investors hold trillions worth in assets, but invest little in green infrastructure.

Current government policy is not supportive enough to accelerate green infrastructure investment. Governments need to pay continued attention to improving the investment environment for private green investment and designing the most cost-effective policies (OECD, 2013n). OECD country surveillance since 2011 has advised countries on green infrastructure investment across the energy, transport and waste sectors. The 2013 Mexican *Economic Survey* (OECD, 2013d), for example, advised Mexico on directing public and private investment into green infrastructure, including in public transportation. Recommendations included improving the planning function and fiscal relations among different government levels and cost-benefit analysis. The 2014 *Economic Survey* of the European Union (OECD, 2014f) recommended streamlining permit procedures to support investment in electricity grids. The OECD has also developed the *Policy Guidance for Investment in Clean Energy Infrastructure* (OECD, 2015d), a non-prescriptive tool that helps governments identify ways to mobilise private-sector investment in clean energy infrastructure. It raises issues for policy makers to consider in the areas of investment policy, investment promotion and facilitation, energy market design, competition policy, financial markets and public governance of energy institutions.

Challenge No. 7: Orienting innovation systems to advance green growth priorities

Innovation is a critical building block for green growth. It is essential to establishing new patterns of production and consumption in order to help decouple growth from natural capital, generate new sources of growth that better reflect the full value of natural capital to society and allow new ways to address environmental risks, and keep transformation costs down. The necessary radical and systemic innovations require greater policy support and related investments.

Governments must gear innovation systems to both accelerate innovation generally and directly promote green technologies.

Government intervention is required to address well-known barriers and drive green innovation. Since many environmental externalities are under-priced – or not priced at all – businesses have little incentive to invest in green innovation. The market for green innovation is also dominated by existing technologies and systems – particularly in energy and transport markets – that create barriers for new entrants (known as lock-in). In addition, market failures, such as difficulties in appropriating returns on investment, generally lead to under-investment. The challenge is to gear innovation systems so that they both accelerate innovation generally and directly promote green technologies and processes, through a "system innovation" approach that addresses specific market failures, but also responds to demand-side issues such as consumer and household acceptance (e.g. through information provision) and institutional resistance (OECD, forthcoming b).

Strong overall framework innovation policies, such as support for basic research and development and protection of intellectual property, are an important but insufficient element of green innovation policy (OECD, forthcoming c). Flexible policy signals that address the externalities associated with environmental challenges are essential in order to generate market demand for green innovation; for example, carbon, water and waste pricing induce potential innovators to seek out the most cost-efficient way to reduce environmental impacts. Well-designed performance standards can also induce innovation. Finally, policy predictability is essential: unpredictable policy signals encourage investors to postpone investments – particularly the risky, non-transferable and capital-intensive investments associated with technological invention and adoption (Criscuolo and Menon, 2014). Targeted innovation-support policies can be challenging to design, due to difficulties in determining technology maturity and future commercial potential. Support for innovation should involve competitive selection processes; it should focus on performance rather than individual technologies, avoid favouring incumbents, ensure rigorous evaluation of policy impacts and contain costs. Governments should embrace a certain degree of trial and error to account for uncertainty when providing discretionary support, providing exit mechanisms when a technology proves unsuccessful, or successful enough to be driven by private actors (Egli, Menon and Johnstone, forthcoming).

Finance's role in inducing innovation is central. Firms engaged in green innovation can find it challenging to access finance, because of the greater commercial risk associated with immature markets, high capital-intensity of some technologies, and relatively long-term investment periods. Recent work demonstrates that the policy context plays an important role in leveraging private finance; the policy context can also enhance merger and acquisition activity in relevant sectors, which can in turn boost finance (Criscuolo et al., 2014). Both public finance and public policies play an important role in mobilising private finance globally (Haščič et al, 2015). The potential of domestic public policies to enhance finance mobilisation to – and in – developing countries in particular remains untapped.

More-tailored policies – e.g. to foster the growth of new entrepreneurial firms and support the transition of small and medium-sized enterprises – are necessary to address specific barriers to innovation. Small and medium-sized enterprises face particular challenges in adopting green innovations and often have weak capacity to demonstrate and commercialise innovations. Policy aiming to reduce their administrative burden and give them access to green public procurement can strengthen capacity. New firms play an important role in delivering increasingly radical innovations that challenge incumbent firms; policy action should support the scaling-up of new business models and facilitate the entry, growth and exit of new firms, by ensuring fair competition and easing access to finance (OECD, 2013; Egli, Menon and Johnstone, forthcoming).

Tailored policies are needed to address specific barriers to green innovation.

While the backbone of innovation policy should be technology-neutral, in practice governments provide discretionary incentives for specific technologies. To the extent possible, such incentives should be evidence-based (Egli, Menon and Johnstone, forthcoming).

R&D expenditure and patents of importance to green growth are two indicators of progress towards green innovation, although measurement is an important issue since "green" innovation can come from a wide variety of domains. For example, biotechnology, (OECD, 2013o) nanotechnology (OECD, 2013p) and information and communications technology have important "environmental" implications, even if the motivation for research in these areas is not seen as such. Public environment-related R&D expenditure has been more or less constant as a share of public R&D spending in OECD countries. The development and diffusion of environmental technologies, as measured through patent data, is generally increasing across countries in all areas of importance to green growth. Yet progress is uneven across countries, and is unlikely to deliver major changes in key environmental domains (OECD, 2014a). Given that a large majority of "green" innovations are developed in a small number of countries, achieving greater global diffusion will be essential.

Openness to the world technology frontier is essential to induce green innovation. Poirier et al. (2015) presents an analysis of the effect of international co-authorship of scientific publications on patenting in wind energy technologies. The results suggest that significant knowledge spillovers exist between OECD countries, but that non-OECD countries particularly benefit from co-operation. This strengthens the case for international research co-operation between OECD and non-OECD countries in the area of climate mitigation. In a related vein, work on water-related climate-adaptation technologies (Dechezlepretre, Haščič and Johnstone, 2015) finds that most innovation worldwide occurs in countries with low or moderate vulnerability to water scarcity. This result highlights the importance of international technology transfer and policies that facilitate broad diffusion of these technologies.

Considerable scope remains for further government action across the breadth of policies required to drive green innovation. OECD country surveillance since 2011 has advised countries on the measures required to drive green innovation, including public support for R&D, targeted support (e.g. aid risk financing and private-sector contributions) and demand-side measures (e.g. innovation-oriented standards and consumer information policies). The reports have also addressed public-private partnerships; support for small and medium-sized enterprises; integrating green innovation in national innovation strategies; and establishing eco-innovation clusters to foster co-operation among government, business and academics. Besides action on the supply and demand sides, improved governance mechanisms and broad stakeholder engagement will be needed to facilitate systemic innovation. More generally, adopting a systemic approach bringing together policy domains that are often kept separate, such as economic (including innovation) policy, environmental and social policies, will also be important.

Challenge No. 8: Accelerating improvements in energy efficiency

Energy efficiency is a fundamental – but largely underutilised – resource for greening the energy sector. Based on current and proposed policies, global energy demand is projected to increase by 37% from 2012 levels by 2040 (IEA, 2014a). The increase would see an associated rise of around 20% in energy-related carbon emissions, consistent with a long-term global mean temperature increase of 3.6°C (degrees Celsius). Further energy-efficiency measures are essential to help relieve the environmental and supply pressures associated with increased energy demand. Average energy-intensity improvements of around 2.4% a year to 2040 are required as part of a portfolio of measures to green the energy sector, consistent with a 2°C target. Such improvements would result in a 15% reduction in global energy demand by 2040 (IEA, 2014a). In addition to energy efficiency, energy supply must be decarbonised to achieve an environmentally and socially sustainable low-carbon energy – particularly electricity – sector.

1.1% boost to global GDP in 2035 by halving energy demand over 2010-2035.

The benefits of energy efficiency are multiple and go well beyond reduced greenhouse gas emissions and energy demand (IEA, 2014d). Halving global primary energy demand over 2010-35 would boost global GDP by an estimated 1.1% in 2035. This effort would require an additional USD 11.8 trillion investment in more efficient end-use technology, but would save more than USD 17.5 trillion in fuel expenditure and USD 5.9 trillion in supply-side investment (Château, Magné and Cozzi, 2014). Energy efficiency can deliver benefits to public budgets, health and well-being, industrial productivity and energy delivery (IEA, 2014d). It stands to reason that these benefits translate at the national level. For example, if Russia were to achieve OECD country energy-efficiency levels, it could sustain current levels of development for decades without supply increases (OECD, 2011d). Mexico loses energy in electricity transmission and distribution at nearly twice the international average rates, wasting around 16% of energy output; increased energy efficiency would help reverse this trend (OECD, 2013d).

Notwithstanding their potential advantages, the bulk of economically viable energy efficiency investments will remain unrealised under current and proposed policies (IEA, 2012). *The Tracking Clean Energy Progress* report produced by the IEA reviews advancement in implementing the low-carbon transition across the energy sector; it notes that energy-efficiency measures are off track in all applicable areas, including buildings, industry, transport, appliances and equipment (IEA, 2014b), despite important policy developments. For example, in June 2014 the United States Environmental Protection Agency proposed a Clean Power Plan to reduce carbon emissions from power plants to 30% below their 2005 levels by 2030 through a number of measures, including more efficient use of electricity; the United States has also introduced stricter building codes and more stringent appliance standards; China is accelerating energy-efficiency measures across its industrial, transport and buildings sectors as part of efforts to reduce local air pollution; India introduced fuel-economy standards for passenger vehicles in 2014; and European Union Member States continue to implement the Energy Efficiency Directive (IEA, 2014c).

Many more measures are needed globally to regulate energy production, distribution and use. Energy efficiency should rely on the standard green growth policy portfolio: pricing mechanisms, to reflect environmental impacts in energy prices; regulatory measures, such as building-efficiency codes and fuel-economy standards; and public awareness and information measures (e.g. labelling and certification programmes, training and education). The measures must be tailored to drive progress across all relevant sectors; sectoral policy in areas such as innovation and finance must also support implementation. OECD country surveillance reports since 2011 present the reach of required policy measures. They provide advice on policies to help finance energy-efficiency improvements; energy metering to guide efficiencies; improving electricity transmission and distribution efficiency; raising public awareness of the benefits of energy efficiency; efficiency certification in the transport sector; measures to drive energy efficiency in buildings; improving national energy-efficiency strategies; developing energy-efficiency indicators; and supporting energy-efficiency improvements in small to medium-sized enterprises.

SUMMING UP THE PARTS

The challenges addressed in this chapter provide useful lessons for governments on ways to accelerate and improve green growth policy implementation. They lead to a number of broader observations related to country experience so far.

- **Almost all OECD countries, and many developing and emerging economies, now use environmentally related taxes to some extent to help achieve environmental objectives. Yet the uptake of pricing mechanisms (such as carbon pricing) directly targeting environmental externalities has proven very challenging,** despite it being more economically efficient to tax externalities directly, rather than inputs or outputs of environmentally damaging activities (e.g. motor vehicle fuels or electricity). Environmentally related taxation currently serves, in this sense, as somewhat of a proxy mechanism for direct pricing of carbon or other externalities associated with electricity generation, transport and other sectors; it also serves as an operating precedent for pricing environmental damage.

- **Much more policy focus and experimentation is needed on how to address political challenges associated with "first-best" pricing mechanisms,** along with rigorous ex post evaluation and rapid dissemination of results (e.g. through case studies). Governments should further focus on regulatory approaches (i.e. beyond their role in addressing areas where price signals are less effective due to market barriers or transaction costs) in jurisdictions where constituencies are strongly opposed to tax increases.

- **In the interim, existing tax mechanisms could be much more effectively oriented to support green growth.** Many countries could shift a significantly higher portion of the tax burden towards environmentally related taxation. Discrepancies and areas of preferential treatment in environmentally related taxation that are not coherent from an environmental perspective – e.g. preferential tax treatment of diesel fuels, insufficient taxation of coal compared to other fuels and tax exemptions for fuel used in agriculture, fishing and forestry – also suggest significant potential for reform. Effective taxation for green growth means looking beyond environmentally related taxation; the current tax treatment of company cars is an example of broader environmentally significant tax policy in need of attention.

- **The discrepancies and misalignments in current tax policy settings demonstrate that governments need to do much more to ensure sectoral policies are aligned to support green growth.** Broad scope to enhance policy in one domain suggests that the potential for reform in other sectors is also great. Further, if intrasectoral policies are not coherent from an environmental perspective, the potential for inconsistencies across sectors and policy portfolios is even greater. Recent work on aligning policies across sectors to transition to a low-carbon economy supports this assumption (Chapter 3).

- **Government subsidy schemes offer vast potential for improved policy alignment.** The USD 640 billion in current government spending on fossil-fuel support dwarfs the amount spent on green technologies and processes, and is incongruous from a green growth perspective. There is scope to improve the effectiveness of green subsidies to ensure they are efficient in driving green growth, retaining the flexibility to adjust to cost reductions while emitting clear market signals. Policy makers should avoid mixed messages, "stop-and-go" policy making and retroactive policy changes.

- **Labour market, skill development and social policies have an important role to play for the structural transformation to unfold smoothly without provoking a political backlash.** General policy support for overall labour market mobility and skill development should be responsive to demand and the training programmes should be continuously adjusted to changing employer demands. As more jobs require more green skills, existing labour and social policy systems should accommodate that shift, just as they adjusted to the demands created by the rapid expansion of information and communications technology. However, the political viability of green growth policies may sometimes require combining ambitious environmental policies with targeted measures to compensate the most visible or politically influential losers from those policies. Ensuring an effective social safety net is particularly essential in developing countries, where populations may be more vulnerable to impacts associated with reform, and transfer systems less developed or non-existent.

- **Gearing sectoral and issue-specific policy to support green growth in investment, energy and beyond will require much more work.** While institutional investors, for example, represent a potentially vast source of finance for green infrastructure projects, current policy settings fail to address the particular challenges they face. Similarly, despite its numerous potential benefits, energy efficiency will remain largely untapped under current policy settings. The measures raised in this chapter provide a potential starting point for reform.

- **Appropriately tailored innovation policies are required.** Innovation is essential to help decouple growth from natural capital depletion and generate new sources of growth. Yet current government policy is unlikely to deliver the breakthrough innovations required in many environmental areas where incremental innovations will not be sufficient to avoid significant environmental damage. The main challenge is to create the right conditions to accelerate innovation generally, and direct innovation more specifically to green technologies and processes through transparent price signals and incentives.

CHAPTER REFERENCES

Ang, G. and V. Marchal (2013), "Mobilising Private Investment in Sustainable Transport: The Case of Land Based Passenger Transport Infrastructure", *OECD Environment Working Papers*, No. 56, OECD Publishing, Paris, http://dx.doi.org/10.1787/5k46hjm8jpmv-en.

Arlinghaus, J. (2015), "Impacts of Carbon Pricing on Indicators of Competitiveness: A Review of Empirical Findings", *OECD Environment Working Papers*, No. 87, OECD Publishing, Paris, http://dx.doi.org/10.1787/5js37p21grzq-en.

Bahar, H., J. Egeland and R. Steenblik (2013), "Domestic Incentive Measures for Renewable Energy with Possible Trade Implications", OECD Trade and Environment Working Papers, No. 2013/01, OECD Publishing, Paris, http://dx.doi.org/10.1787/5k44srlksr6f-en.

Banister, D., P. Crist and S. Perkins (2015), "Land Transport and How to Unlock Investment in Support of "Green Growth", *OECD Green Growth Papers*, No. 2015/01, OECD Publishing, Paris, http://dx.doi.org/10.1787/5js65xnk52kc-en.

Beltramello, A., L. Haie-Fayle and D. Pilat (2013), "Why New Business Models Matter for Green Growth", *OECD Green Growth Papers*, No. 2013/01, OECD Publishing, Paris, http://dx.doi.org/10.1787/5k97gk40v3ln-en.

Château, J., B. Magné and L. Cozzi (2014), "Economic Implications of the IEA Efficient World Scenario", *OECD Environment Working Papers*, No. 64, OECD Publishing, Paris, http://dx.doi.org/10.1787/5jz2qcn29lbw-en.

Convery, F. J., L. Dunne and D. Joyce (2013), "Ireland's Carbon Tax and the Fiscal Crisis: Issues in Fiscal Adjustment, Environmental Effectiveness, Competitiveness, Leakage and Equity Implications", *OECD Environment Working Papers*, No. 59, OECD Publishing, Paris, http://dx.doi.org/10.1787/5k3z11j3w0bw-en.

Corfee-Morlot, J. et al. (2012), "Towards a Green Investment Policy Framework: The Case of Low-Carbon, Climate-Resilient Infrastructure", *OECD Environment Working Papers*, No. 48, OECD Publishing, Paris, http://dx.doi.org/10.1787/5k8zth7s6s6d-en.

Criscuolo, C. and C. Menon (2014), "Environmental Policies and Risk Finance in the Green Sector: Cross-country Evidence", *OECD Science, Technology and Industry Working Papers*, No. 2014/01, OECD Publishing, Paris, http://dx.doi.org/10.1787/5jz6wn918j37-en.

Criscuolo, C. et al. (2014), "Renewable Energy Policies and Cross-border Investment: Evidence from Mergers and Acquisitions in Solar and Wind Energy", *OECD Science, Technology and Industry Working Papers*, No. 2014/03, OECD Publishing, Paris, http://dx.doi.org/10.1787/5jxv9f3r9623-en.

Dechezleprêtre, A., I. Haščič and N. Johnstone (2015), "Invention and International Diffusion of Water Conservation and Availability Technologies: Evidence from Patent Data", *OECD Environment Working Papers*, No. 82, OECD Publishing, Paris, http://dx.doi.org/10.1787/5js679fvllhg-en.

Egli, F., C. Menon and N. Johnstone (forthcoming), "Quality and Breakthrough Inventions: The Case of Climate Mitigation Technologies" *OECD Science, Technology and Industry Working Papers*, OECD Publishing, Paris.

European Commission (2011), *Proposal for a Council Directive Amending Directive 2003/96/EC restructuring the Community framework for the taxation of energy products and electricity*, European Commission, http://ec.europa.eu/taxation_customs/resources/documents/taxation/com_2011_169_en.pdf.

Greene, J. and N. A. Braathen (2014), "Tax Preferences for Environmental Goals: Use, Limitations and Preferred Practices", *OECD Environment Working Papers*, No. 71, OECD Publishing, Paris, http://dx.doi.org/10.1787/5jxwrr4hkd6l-en.

Harding, M. (2014a), "The Diesel Differential: Differences in the Tax Treatment of Gasoline and Diesel for Road Use", *OECD Taxation Working Papers*, No. 21, OECD Publishing, Paris, http://dx.doi.org/10.1787/5jz14cd7hk6b-en.

Harding, M. (2014b), "Personal Tax Treatment of Company Cars and Commuting Expenses: Estimating the Fiscal and Environmental Costs", *OECD Taxation Working Papers*, No. 20, OECD Publishing, Paris, http://dx.doi.org/10.1787/5jz14cg1s7vl-en.

Harrison, K. (2013), "The Political Economy of British Columbia's Carbon Tax", *OECD Environment Working Papers*, No. 63, OECD Publishing, Paris, http://dx.doi.org/10.1787/5k3z04gkkhkg-en.

Haščič, I. et al. (2015), "Public Interventions and Private Climate Finance Flows: Empirical Evidence from Renewable Energy Financing", *OECD Environment Working Papers*, No. 80, OECD Publishing, Paris, http://dx.doi.org/10.1787/5js6b1r9lfd4-en.

Kaminker, C. et al. (2013), "Institutional Investors and Green Infrastructure Investments: Selected Case Studies", *OECD Working Papers on Finance, Insurance and Private Pensions*, No. 35, OECD Publishing, Paris, http://dx.doi.org/10.1787/5k3xr8k6jb0n-en.

Kennedy, C and J. Corfee-Morlot (2013), "Past performance and future needs for low carbon climate resilient infrastructure – An investment perspective", *Energy Policy*, Vol. 59, pp. 773-783, www.sciencedirect.com/science/article/pii/S0301421513002814.

IEA (2014a), *Energy Technology Perspectives 2014*, IEA, Paris, http://dx.doi.org/10.1787/energy_tech-2014-en.

IEA (2014b), *Tracking Clean Energy Progress 2014*, IEA, Paris, www.iea.org/publications/freepublications/publication/Tracking_clean_energy_progress_2014.pdf.

IEA (2014c), *World Energy Outlook 2014*, IEA, Paris, http://dx.doi.org/10.1787/weo-2014-en.

IEA (2014d), *Capturing the Multiple Benefits of Energy Efficiency: A Guide to Quantifying the Value Added*, IEA, Paris, http://dx.doi.org/10.1787/9789264220720-en.

IEA (2012), *World Energy Outlook 2012*, IEA, Paris, http://www.worldenergyoutlook.org/publications/weo-2012/.

New Climate Economy (2014), *New Climate Economy Report*, http://newclimateeconomy.report/.

OECD/ECLAC (2014), *OECD Environmental Performance Reviews: Colombia 2014*, OECD Publishing, Paris, http://dx.doi.org/10.1787/9789264208292-en.

OECD/ITF (2013), *Better Regulation of Public-Private Partnerships for Transport Infrastructure*, ITF Round Tables, No. 151, OECD Publishing, Paris/ITF, Paris, http://dx.doi.org/10.1787/9789282103951-en.

OECD (forthcoming a), "Overcoming Barriers to International Investment in Clean Energy", OECD Publishing, Paris, http://dx.doi.org/10.1787/9789264227064-en.

OECD (forthcoming b), "System Innovation", OECD Publishing, Paris.

OECD (forthcoming c), "Strengthening Innovation – Policy Strategies and their Implementation", OECD Publishing, Paris.

OECD (2015a), *Material Resources, Productivity and the Environment*, OECD Green Growth Studies, OECD Publishing, Paris, http://dx.doi.org/10.1787/9789264190504-en.

OECD (2015b), *OECD Economic Surveys: Indonesia 2015*, OECD Publishing, Paris, http://dx.doi.org/10.1787/eco_surveys-idn-2015-en.

OECD (2015c), *Mapping Channels to Mobilise Institutional Investment in Sustainable Energy*, Green Finance and Investment, OECD Publishing, Paris, http://dx.doi.org/10.1787/9789264224582-en.

OECD (2015d), *Policy Guidance for Investment in Clean Energy Infrastructure: Expanding Access to Clean Energy for Green Growth and Development*, OECD Publishing, Paris, http://dx.doi.org/10.1787/9789264212664-en.

OECD (2014a), *Green Growth Indicators 2014*, OECD Green Growth Studies, OECD Publishing, Paris, http://dx.doi.org/10.1787/9789264202030-en.

OECD (2014b), *OECD Economic Surveys: Australia 2014*, OECD Publishing, Paris, http://dx.doi.org/10.1787/eco_surveys-aus-2014-en.

OECD (2014c), *OECD Economic Surveys: Spain 2014*, OECD Publishing, Paris, http://dx.doi.org/10.1787/eco_surveys-esp-2014-en.

OECD (2014d), "Report on the Implementation of the Recommendation of the Council on Resource Productivity [C(2008)40/CORR1]", C(2014)148/CORR1, OECD, Paris.
OECD (2014e), *The Cost of Air Pollution: Health Impacts of Road Transport,* OECD Publishing, Paris, http://dx.doi.org/10.1787/9789264210448-en.
OECD (2014f), *OECD Economic Surveys: European Union 2014,* OECD Publishing, Paris, http://dx.doi.org/10.1787/eco_surveys-eur-2014-en.
OECD (2014g), *OECD Economic Surveys: India 2014,* OECD Publishing, Paris, http://dx.doi.org/10.1787/eco_surveys-ind-2014-en.
OECD (2014h), *Annual Survey of Large Pension Funds and Public Pension Reserve Funds: Report on Pension Funds' Long-Term Investments,* www.oecd.org/daf/fin/private-pensions/2014_Large_Pension_Funds_Survey.pdf.
OECD (2013a), *Effective Carbon Prices,* OECD Publishing, Paris, http://dx.doi.org/10.1787/9789264196964-en.
OECD (2013b), *OECD Economic Surveys: Austria 2013,* OECD Publishing, Paris, http://dx.doi.org/10.1787/eco_surveys-aut-2013-en.
OECD (2013c), *OECD Environmental Performance Reviews: Italy 2013,* OECD Publishing, Paris, http://dx.doi.org/10.1787/9789264186378-en.
OECD (2013d), *OECD Economic Surveys: Mexico 2013,* OECD Publishing, Paris, http://dx.doi.org/10.1787/eco_surveys-mex-2013-en.
OECD (2013e), *OECD Economic Surveys: New Zealand 2013,* OECD Publishing, Paris, http://dx.doi.org/10.1787/eco_surveys-nzl-2013-en.
OECD (2013f), *OECD Economic Surveys: South Africa 2013,* OECD Publishing, Paris, http://dx.doi.org/10.1787/eco_surveys-zaf-2013-en.
OECD (2013g), *OECD Economic Surveys: Belgium 2013,* OECD Publishing, Paris, http://dx.doi.org/10.1787/eco_surveys-bel-2013-en.
OECD (2013h), *Taxing Energy Use: A Graphical Analysis,* OECD Publishing, Paris, http://dx.doi.org/10.1787/9789264183933-en.
OECD (2013i), *OECD Economic Surveys: China 2013,* OECD Publishing, Paris, http://dx.doi.org/10.1787/eco_surveys-chn-2013-en.
OECD (2013j), *OECD Economic Surveys: France 2013,* OECD Publishing, Paris, http://dx.doi.org/10.1787/eco_surveys-fra-2013-en.
OECD (2013k), *OECD Economic Surveys: Japan 2013,* OECD Publishing, Paris, http://dx.doi.org/10.1787/eco_surveys-jpn-2013-en.
OECD (2013l), *OECD Investment Policy Reviews: Jordan 2013,* OECD Publishing, Paris, http://dx.doi.org/10.1787/9789264202276-en.
OECD (2013m), *Inventory of Estimated Budgetary Support and Tax Expenditures for Fossil Fuels 2013,* OECD Publishing, Paris, http://dx.doi.org/10.1787/9789264187610-en.
OECD (2013n), *2013 Green Growth and Sustainable Development Forum summary,* OECD, Paris, http://www.oecd.org/greengrowth/green-development/Summary%20GGSD%202013%20final.pdf.
OECD (2013o), "Biotechnology for the Environment in the Future: Science, Technology and Policy", *OECD Science, Technology and Industry Policy Papers,* No. 3, OECD Publishing, Paris, http://dx.doi.org/10.1787/5k4840hqhp7j-en.
OECD (2013p), "Nanotechnology for Green Innovation", *OECD Science, Technology and Industry Policy Papers,* No. 5, OECD Publishing, Paris, http://dx.doi.org/10.1787/5k450q9j8p8q-en.
OECD (2012a), *Meeting the Water Reform Challenge,* OECD Studies on Water, OECD Publishing, Paris, http://dx.doi.org/10.1787/9789264170001-en.
OECD (2012b), *OECD Economic Surveys: Australia 2012,* OECD Publishing, Paris, http://dx.doi.org/10.1787/eco_surveys-aus-2012-en.
OECD (2012c), *OECD Environmental Performance Reviews: Germany 2012,* OECD Publishing, Paris, http://dx.doi.org/10.1787/9789264169302-en.
OECD (2012d), *OECD Economic Surveys: Portugal 2012,* OECD Publishing, Paris, http://dx.doi.org/10.1787/eco_surveys-prt-2012-en.
OECD (2012e), *OECD Economic Surveys: Poland 2012,* OECD Publishing, Paris, http://dx.doi.org/10.1787/eco_surveys-pol-2012-en.
OECD (2011a), *OECD Economic Surveys: Belgium 2011,* OECD Publishing, Paris, http://dx.doi.org/10.1787/eco_surveys-bel-2011-en.
OECD (2011b), *OECD Environmental Performance Reviews: Israel 2011,* OECD Publishing, Paris, http://dx.doi.org/10.1787/9789264117563-en.
OECD (2011c), *OECD Economic Surveys: Ireland 2011,* OECD Publishing, Paris, http://dx.doi.org/10.1787/eco_surveys-irl-2011-en.
OECD (2011d), *OECD Economic Surveys: Russian Federation 2011,* OECD Publishing, Paris, http://dx.doi.org/10.1787/eco_surveys-rus-2011-en.
Poirier, J. et al. (2015), "The Benefits of International Co-authorship in Scientific Papers: The Case of Wind Energy Technologies", *OECD Environment Working Papers,* No. 81, OECD Publishing, Paris, http://dx.doi.org/10.1787/5js69ld9w9nv-en.
Roy, R. (2014), "Environmental and Related Social Costs of the Tax Treatment of Company Cars and Commuting Expenses", *OECD Environment Working Papers,* No. 70, OECD Publishing, Paris, http://dx.doi.org/10.1787/5jxwrr5163zp-en.
Sovereign Wealth Funds Institute (2015), "Sovereign Wealth Fund Ranking", http://www.swfinstitute.org/fund-rankings/.
World Bank (2014), *State and Trends of Carbon Pricing 2014,* World Bank, Washington, DC, http://documents.worldbank.org/curated/en/2014/05/19572833/state-trends-carbon-pricing-2014.

1 Based on responses to a high-level survey issued to OECD member countries and key partner economies in October 2014.
2 Of the 115 publications considered for this report – i.e. those published between the Green Growth Strategy's launch and 4 February 2015 – 80 include green growth-relevant recommendations. Together, the reviews make 310 relevant recommendations. *Economic Surveys* are available at www.oecd.org/eco/surveys/; *Environmental Performance Reviews* at www.oecd.org/env/country-reviews/; and *Investment Policy Reviews at* http://www.oecd.org/investment/countryreviews.htm. *Reviews of Innovation Policy* (www.oecd.org/science/inno/oecdreviewsofinnovationpolicy.htm) were also considered, but the series does not currently advise on green growth issues.
3 www.whitehouse.gov/the-press-office/2014/11/11/us-china-joint-announcement-climate-change.
4 The evidence is insufficient to give a precise estimate of the road transport proportion of these costs, but it is likely considerable.
5 OECD database of instruments used for environmental policy.
6 The OECD is currently undertaking work to analyse the structure and level of taxes on energy use in OECD partner economies. This work will be released in 2015 as part of an update to the OECD (2013), *Taxing Energy Use: A Graphical Analysis,* OECD Publishing, Paris.
7 26 of 34 OECD countries were considered in Harding (2014), "Personal Tax Treatment of Company Cars and Commuting Expenses: Estimating the Fiscal and Environmental Costs", *OECD Taxation Working Papers,* No. 20, OECD Publishing. Company cars comprise around one-fifth of the passenger car fleet in Belgium, for example *(OECD Economic Surveys: Belgium 2011),* around one-half of new passenger cars in Poland, and one-third in each of Germany and Mexico *(OECD Economic Surveys: Poland 2012; OECD Economic Surveys: Germany 2012; OECD Economic Surveys: Mexico 2013).*
8 An update to the inventory (forthcoming) will also cover six OECD partner economies: Brazil, China, India, Indonesia, Russia and South Africa.
9 Excluding vehicles. Building investment is also not included in these figures.

CHAPTER 3

REVISITING THE GREEN GROWTH STRATEGY

This chapter surveys the considerable volume of OECD work relevant to green growth undertaken since release of the Green Growth Strategy in 2011, representing more than 130 OECD sectoral and issue-specific publications across virtually all applicable policy areas. Based on this work, as well as country experience to date (Chapter 2), the chapter proposes five enhancements to the Green Growth Strategy, to help ease country implementation, give renewed vigour and direction to country efforts, and provide an updated framework to guide policy work. The chapter concludes by proposing a number of forward work priorities related to green growth for governments, the OECD and other relevant institutions.

Work since 2011 suggests a number of enhancements to the Green Growth Strategy. Better understanding of the links between economic and environmental goals and increased emphasis on public trust in reform are priority areas.

The Green Growth Strategy in 2015: strengthening the OECD framework advice on green growth. OECD green growth work has significantly expanded since the launch of the Green Growth Strategy, consistent with the work programme proposed in 2011. More than 130 sectoral and issue-specific publications relevant to green growth have been released across virtually all applicable policy areas. This chapter examines the analysis performed since 2011 and considers how it might be used to update and enrich the strategy. What does a "comprehensive" policy approach to conserving natural capital while driving economic growth look like in 2015, bearing in mind that work on green growth policy design is ongoing? The chapter maps the work undertaken since 2011 against the advice provided at that time, across the four steps outlined in the Green Growth Strategy. It considers how country experience since 2011 (as outlined in Chapter 2) might inform the strategy to help ease country implementation. The intention is to provide renewed vigour and direction to country efforts, as well as an updated framework to guide policy work.

ADVISING ON GREEN GROWTH ACROSS THE ECONOMY: WORK SINCE 2011

How has green growth analysis advanced since 2011? Table 3.1 captures the major analytical outcomes of work undertaken by the OECD since 2011. It first addresses work to support aligning growth and environmental objectives. Important analysis is emerging that aims to help governments better understand the linkages, complementarities and trade-offs between economic and environmental goals and begin to answer a number of questions, such as how – if at all – environmental regulation impacts economic growth, and what sorts of feedbacks environmental degradation is likely to have on the economy. Next, it addresses green growth policy frameworks. Work to provide more targeted insights into greening growth with respect to specific sectors and issues is advancing in several areas, e.g., efforts to understand the costs and benefits of various policy instruments (i.e. pricing mechanisms, green subsidies) and to accelerate fossil-fuel subsidy reform. Additional effort is still required in other areas.

Considerably less attention has been paid to advancing analytical work on the social and labour implications of green growth. Work in this area, addressed third, has mainly focused on skills and local-level issues, with some work on evidence of the distributional effects of energy taxes and economic modelling of the potential impacts of fossil-fuel subsidy reform on the poorest households. The OECD Green Growth and Sustainable Development Forum addressed the social impacts of green growth in 2014 as a gap in the green growth analysis. Other work has touched on the potential competitiveness impacts of reform, also described. Work to advance green growth indicators is the final item. Development of the OECD green growth indicators continues following the release of Green Growth Indicators 2014 (OECD, 2014a), updating the initial set of indicators included as part of the 2011 Green Growth Strategy.

TABLE 3.1 – DEVELOPMENT OF OECD ANALYSIS ON GREEN GROWTH 2011-15

1. ALIGN GROWTH AND ENVIRONMENTAL OBJECTIVES	
2011 Green Growth Strategy advice	**Development in advice since 2011**
▪ **Gear core economic policies to mutually reinforce growth and natural capital conservation** · Determine country-level environmental priorities: assess long-term environmental conditions and risks, and least-cost policy options and areas for intervention, underpinned by cost-benefit analysis · Link environmental objectives to economic reform priorities to achieve green growth objectives · Anchor green growth in core economic ministries and drive cross-portfolio co-ordination · Address constraints to green investment and innovation	▪ **Increasing the stringency of environmental policies does not harm productivity levels; in fact, tightening environmental policy stringency is associated with a subsequent short-run boost in productivity growth, with negligible net effect in the medium run.** Market-based instruments tend to have a more robust positive effect on productivity growth (Albrizio, Koźluk and Zipperer, 2014). · **Over 1990-2012,** environmental policy became more stringent in OECD countries, as demonstrated by a new Environmental Policy Stringency Indicator, with no negative effect on growth (Botta and Koźluk, 2014). ▪ **Inaction on environmental and natural capital degradation will likely have significant impacts on economic growth in the coming decades;** for example, global gross domestic product (GDP) impacts from climate change alone are projected to increase more rapidly than growth, resulting in gradually increasing GDP loss (Dellink et al., 2014): · **1-3.3%** projected global GDP loss by 2060 from limited modelled climate change effects, with much larger variations in consequences on specific sectors and regions ▪ **The economic cost of outdoor air pollution in terms of the value of lives lost and ill health is much higher than previously thought** (OECD, 2014b): · **USD 1.7 trillion** (US dollars) estimated cost in OECD countries, 2010, around half attributable to pollution from road transport · **USD 1.3 and 0.5 trillion** estimated cost in China and India · **4% of GDP** social cost of outdoor air pollution in OECD countries on average, ranging up to 10% · **12% and 9% of GDP**, estimated social cost for China and India respectively, 2005 · **4% increase** in premature deaths globally caused by outdoor air pollution, 2005-10.  ▪ **The scope to improve ex ante and ex post assessments of policy proposals (and investment projects) through more, and better, use of cost-benefit analysis, including economic valuation of environmental externalities, is great is great (forthcoming OECD work).** · While clear guidelines for use of cost-benefit analysis regarding energy and transport investment exist in a number of countries, they are less common for general ex ante policy assessments, and almost non-existent for ex post assessments of policies or projects. · "Values of statistical lives" should be included for assessments where mortality impacts play an important role (OECD, 2012a). 

2. IMPLEMENT GREEN GROWTH POLICY FRAMEWORKS

Policy packages to price pollution and provide incentives for efficient resource use

2011 advice	Development in advice since 2011
▪ **Implement:** ▫ **Pricing instruments** to drive broad-based, least-cost action, efficiency and innovation (tradable permit systems, taxes) ▫ **Price pollution, encourage efficient resource use and innovation, and help drive growth** by increasing environmentally related taxation and shifting the tax burden away from more distortive taxes (i.e. on labour), thus contributing to fiscal consolidation ▫ **Tax pollution as directly as possible** (e.g. carbon emissions) rather than inputs or outputs of environmentally damaging activities, for economic efficiency. ▫ **Regulation** to provide incentives for green growth (emissions performance standards, energy efficiency) ▫ **Subsidies** to promote green technologies, products and practices; fossil-fuel subsidy reform ▫ **Eliminate environmentally perverse subsidies** to help shift the balance of incentives towards environmentally sound products and practices ▫ **Information measures** to guide consumer behaviour	▪ **Empirical evidence supports the traditional textbook claim that pricing instruments (i.e. tradable permit systems, taxes) are cost-effective in reducing carbon emissions when compared with other policy instruments** (OECD, 2013a), although further objectives of other instruments (e.g. technology development and demonstration, and cost reduction) must also be taken into account. ▫ **15 countries and 5 sectors surveyed** (for electricity generation, road transport, pulp and paper and cement, and domestic energy use) ▪ **The structure and level of taxes on energy use – which represent 72% of environmentally related tax revenue in OECD countries – are not environmentally coherent in many countries.** This suggests significant untapped, low-cost opportunity for reform (OECD, 2013b). ▫ **33 of 34** OECD countries tax diesel at lower rates than gasoline, despite greater environmental and social externalities (Harding, 2014a). ▪ **Green growth-relevant tax policy goes beyond environmentally related taxation:** the tax treatment of company cars is one example (Roy, 2014; Harding, 2014b). ▫ **26.8 EUR billion** fiscal cost per year due to favourable tax treatment of company cars for personal purposes in all OECD countries; **116 EUR billion** associated social costs, including due to increased local pollution ▪ **Tax preferences (e.g. reduced tax rates or exemptions) are not helpful to address negative environmental externalities;** environmental taxes should be used instead. ▫ Preferences retain a role to support positive externalities (i.e. delivery of greater social benefits than would otherwise be the case, through for example government support for R&D) (Greene and Braathen, 2014). ▪ **Large-scale, environmentally harmful support for fossil fuels – incongruent from a green growth perspective – remains prevalent and globally substantial,** with USD 640 billion in annual government funding (OECD, 2013c; IEA, 2014a). ▫ **More than 550** identified measures support use or production of fossil fuels in OECD countries, with an estimated overall value of **USD 90 billion** a year, through measures such as direct transfers, risk assumption and preferential tax treatment. ▫ **USD 550 billion** spent annually by emerging and developing countries alone on support for consumption.

Gear issue- and sector-specific policy for green growth

2011 advice	Development in advice since 2011
▪ **Align sectoral policy** to support green growth and remove any barriers or distortions in existing frameworks	▪ **Several misalignments in existing policy frameworks currently hinder the transition to a low-carbon economy, driving home the need for governments to look across policy areas in implementing green growth (OECD, forthcoming a).** ▫ Identified misalignments arise in investment, taxation, innovation and international trade, as well as from the perspective of policy governing specific areas such as electricity systems, urban mobility and rural land use.

2. IMPLEMENT GREEN GROWTH POLICY FRAMEWORKS INVESTMENT AND FINANCE

Gear issue- and sector-specific policy for green growth

2011 advice	Development in advice since 2011
▪ **Scale up investment in green infrastructure** through clear, long-term policy signals on the need to reduce pollution and enhance resource efficiency, as well as measures to facilitate investment by major institutional investors	▪ **The green investment challenge may be more about channelling investment towards the right kind of infrastructure than unlocking significant amounts of additional capital (OECD, 2013d)** · **USD 2 trillion** is invested annually in infrastructure (energy, water and transport sectors, excluding vehicles), with an additional **USD 1.2 trillion** a year invested to 2030 to develop and maintain current levels of infrastructure capacity and service. · **USD 450 billion, or an estimated 14%** in potential savings from system-wide efficiency gains from green investment (Kennedy and Corfee-Morlot, 2013). · **USD 44 trillion** additional investment to decarbonise the energy system in line with international climate goals will yield savings of **USD 71 trillion** by 2050 (IEA, 2014b). ▪ **Given the scale of investment needed as well as current strains on public finances, engaging private-sector investment is essential (OECD, 2015a).** · Examining existing rules, regulations and policies that may restrict investment in green infrastructure, creating investment vehicles that generate required risk-return ratios (OECD, 2015b), promoting collaborative dialogue among investors and government, and compiling and sharing data to evaluate the risk and performance of investments are relevant (Kaminker et al., 2013), in addition to core green growth policy settings (e.g. pricing pollution and natural-resource use, eliminating fossil-fuel subsidies, and strengthening core investment and competition policy). ▪ **Institutional investors are a promising source of finance, but currently invest little in green infrastructure projects due to the particular challenges they face,** such as lack of expertise in direct infrastructure investment, diversification and exposure limits, and minimum scale for projects. · **USD 93 trillion** in assets were held by institutional investors such as insurance companies, investment funds and pension funds in OECD countries in 2013 (OECD, 2015b); only **1%** of large pension fund assets were allocated directly to infrastructure projects of all types in 2013. Allocation to green infrastructure investment was estimated to be much smaller, at only **3% of that 1%** share. ▪ **Policy is required to address the specific challenges faced by institutional investors (OECD, 2015b).** · Potential measures to catalyse further investment include establishing a national infrastructure strategy and road map, facilitating the development and application of risk mitigants, reducing the transaction costs associated with sustainable energy investment, and establishing a dedicated green investment bank.

2. IMPLEMENT GREEN GROWTH POLICY FRAMEWORKS INNOVATION

Gear issue- and sector-specific policy for green growth

2011 advice	Development in advice since 2011
Drive innovation to help decouple growth from natural capital depletion, generate new sources of growth and find new ways to address environmental risks, through policy that: - Prices environmental externalities - Addresses barriers to early-stage technology development, demonstration and deployment, through targeted support and demand-side policies (e.g. regulation, public procurement) - Accounts for the needs of new, entrepreneurial firms and small and medium-sized enterprises - Accelerates diffusion and adoption of green innovation.	**The backbone of innovation policy should be technology-neutral, but targeted direct support measures are an important complement.** - While criteria used to identify specific technology areas is an open research question, early work indicates that the broad economic applicability of technologies in a variety of sectors is an important indicator that may assist governments wishing to provide discretionary incentives for specific technologies, given finite budgets (Egli, Menon and Johnstone, forthcoming). **Provided they are not so generous as to raise concerns about fiscal sustainability, targeted supply-side policies and demand-side measures promote higher levels of finance for firms engaged in green innovation –** which often find it challenging to access finance because of the greater commercial risk associated with immature markets, regulatory uncertainty associated with potential changes to environmental policy, etc. – than shorter-term fiscal policies such as tax incentives and rebates (Criscuolo and Menon, 2014). They can also enhance merger and acquisition activity in relevant sectors, which can in turn boost finance (Criscuolo et al., 2014). **New firms play an important role in delivering more radical innovations that challenge incumbent firms; policy action is needed to support the scale-up of new business models and facilitate the entry, exit and growth of new firms,** including by ensuring fair competition and easing access to finance (Beltramello, Haie-Fayle and Pilat, 2013). **Openness to the world technology frontier is essential to maximise the benefits of green innovation.** - This includes international co-operation in scientific research (Poirier et al., 2015) and openness to technology transfer (Dechezleprêtre, Haščič and Johnstone, 2015). OECD countries and partner economies co-operate intensely, providing considerable benefits for global and regional public goods.

TRADE AND FOREIGN DIRECT INVESTMENT

2011 advice	Development in advice since 2011
Respect basic trade and investment law principles, such as avoiding protectionist measures like local content requirements, to facilitate development and global diffusion of green technologies, and required foreign direct investment	**Policies aiming to favour domestic manufacturers in the renewable-energy and electric vehicle sectors are increasing, particularly in non-OECD countries, and represent a barrier to international trade and investment in green infrastructure.** Local content requirements, for example, increase the cost and decelerate market penetration by clean energy technologies; alternative policies should be favoured (e.g. policies targeted at the business and regulatory environment, trade and investment barriers, and helping domestic producers identify ways to plug into global value chains) (Bahar, Egeland and Steenblik, 2013; OECD 2015c; OECD forthcoming b). - **21** local content requirements related to renewable energy have been planned or implemented in OECD countries and emerging economies since the financial crisis. - **Several** World Trade Organization disputes have been associated with the use of local content requirements in solar and wind energy since 2010.

2. IMPLEMENT GREEN GROWTH POLICY FRAMEWORKS
ENERGY

Gear issue- and sector-specific policy for green growth

2011 advice	Development in advice since 2011
Transition the energy system away from, and avoid locking in, polluting and carbon-intensive energy infrastructure, through policies to drive deployment of a portfolio of sustainable energy technologies	**Contributions from all sectors and a portfolio of technologies will be needed to transform energy supply and end use to address energy-related environmental impacts,** as well as energy security and cost concerns, while meeting growing energy demand. Energy efficiency (38%), renewables (30%) and carbon capture and storage (14%) make up the largest contributions to global emissions reductions in a scenario to 2050, but nuclear power, end-use fuel-switching, and efficiency and fuel-switching for power generation remain essential (IEA, 2014b). Future projections are as follows:

- **70%** projected increase in global energy demand in 2050 from 2011 levels based on current policies, with **60%** associated increase in carbon emission levels
- **25%** energy demand growth in 2050, as constrained by strategic policy action consistent with a sustainable energy system, with associated emissions reductions of **50%** from 2011.

Figure 1.3 Contributions to annual emissions reductions between the 6DS and 2DS

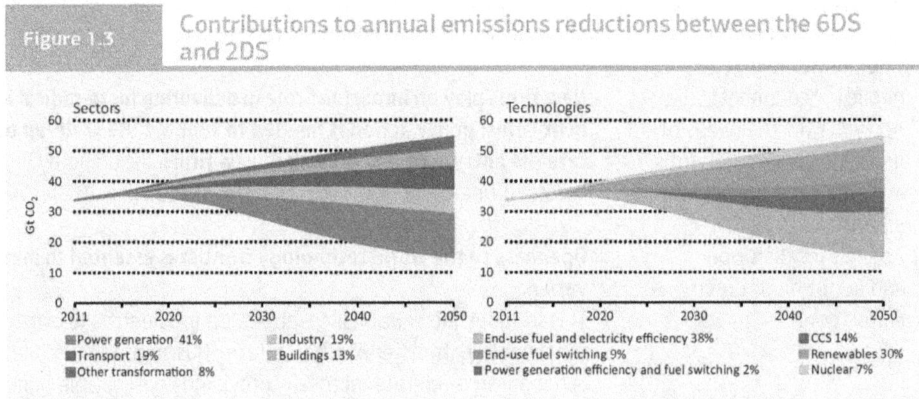

- **Political and financial commitment to long-term sustainability of the global energy system is inadequate;** while the deployment of solar photovoltaic modules, onshore wind turbines and electric vehicles is increasing rapidly, growth of coal-fired power generation continues to exceed that of all non-fossil fuels combined, nuclear power generation is stagnating, and development of carbon capture and storage remains too slow; a series of policy measures is required to accelerate progress across energy technologies.
  - **5.5%** annual growth rate in renewable power generation between 2006-13, up from 3% a year in 2000-06; expected **40%** growth rate between 2013-18 (**5.8%** a year) (IEA, 2014c)
  - **50%** growth rate in electric vehicle sales between 2012-13
  - **52%** increase in coal-fired electricity generation between 2000-11, compared with around **25%** growth in generation from non-fossil energy sources
  - **7%** decrease in global nuclear power generation between 2011-12
  - **55 million tonnes** of carbon stored with monitoring so far; 226 million tonnes to be captured and stored per year by 2025 in a sustainable energy system scenario.

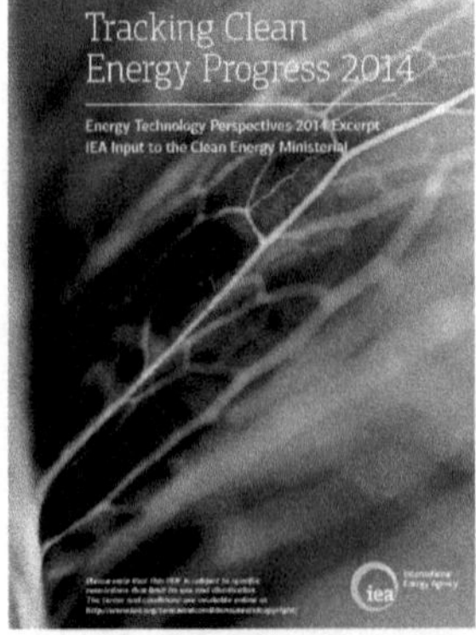

- **Overarching opportunities for policy action include innovation, radically improving energy efficiency and implementing systems-based energy strategies** (OECD, 2012b), but tailored policies are needed to advance the transition across energy technologies (IEA, 2014d).

2. IMPLEMENT GREEN GROWTH POLICY FRAMEWORKS

TRANSPORT

Gear issue- and sector-specific policy for green growth

2011 advice

- **Transport infrastructure investment will shape activity and demand well into the future; policies need to be guided by robust cost-benefit analysis** that considers the long-term economic, environmental and social impacts
- **To reduce carbon intensity of travel, initial focus should be on improving the fuel efficiency of conventional engines,** then gradually introducing alternative technologies, fuel types and energy carriers

Development in advice since 2011

- **Policies need to be aligned to manage urban sprawl, establish higher fuel prices and prioritise the expansion of public transport infrastructure;** integration and alignment of policies is also most effective in addressing climate and health objectives (OECD/ITF, 2015). Projections are as follows:
  - **240% to 450%** increase in passenger transport in non-OECD countries to 2050
  - **230% to 420%** growth in world road and rail freight volumes to 2050
  - **30% to 40%** possible reduction of CO_2 emissions through public transport-oriented policies in Latin American, Chinese and Indian cities.
- **The government has a strong role to play** in funding infrastructure, subsidising new technologies (initially), guaranteeing investment (risk sharing) and providing the necessary stability to build investor confidence through clear and consistent messages (OECD/ITF, 2015).
  - **20%-25% of GDP** is invested in transportation, with levels declining in developed countries and rising in emerging economies.
- **Large institutional investors**, such as pension funds and sovereign wealth funds with long-term liabilities and a low risk appetite, are ideally suited to invest in transportation infrastructure assets.

AGRICULTURE

2011 advice

- **Assess and eliminate agricultural subsidies that run counter to the objectives of green growth** (e.g. by distorting signals that would otherwise improve global agricultural productivity)

Development in advice since 2011

- **Tailored green growth indicators are needed to help track the transition to a low-carbon, resource-efficient agriculture sector.**
  - **25 preliminary indicators** exist to assess green growth progress in agriculture (OECD, 2014c)
- **OECD countries are making progress in reducing agriculture subsidies** (OECD, 2013e), with a resulting
  - **85%** drop in total support over **1990-92 and 49%** drop in 2009-12, but an increase in environmentally beneficial support from 1% to 8% over the same period (2009-12).
- **Ongoing long-term investment in innovation and R&D is essential** in order to improve agricultural productivity, reduce environmental impacts and increase competitiveness (OECD, 2013e).
- **Advisory, training and extension measures constitute a vital element in supporting the transition towards sustainable agriculture,** resulting in investment returns, gains in productivity and improved environmental performance (OECD, forthcoming c).
  - **Measures should be targeted and have clear objectives within the policy mix** – credibility, relevance and up-to-date business-acumen advice, training and extension are the key requirements for persuading farmers to adopt practices to foster green growth.

2. IMPLEMENT GREEN GROWTH POLICY FRAMEWORKS
WATER

Gear issue- and sector-specific policy for green growth

2011 advice	Development in advice since 2011
Protect and restore surface and ground water bodies, and ensure appropriate public access to safe drinking water and wastewater treatment, through investment in water infrastructure and reduced pollution discharges (i.e. through wastewater treatment and integrating water quality considerations into agricultural and other sectoral policies)	**Sustainable finance is essential to ensure environmental sustainability of water ecosystems, reduce flood and drought impacts, and maximise access to water supply and sanitation.** Several countries have advanced financing mechanisms (e.g. tariffs, user charges, pollution charges and water markets). Private financing, establishing measures to overcome multilevel governance challenges, and aligning water and other sectoral policies (e.g. energy and agri-environmental policies) are among the further measures required (OECD, 2012c). - **0.35-1.2% GDP** is needed every year for the next 20 years to modernise and upgrade water systems in OECD countries. - **USD 54 billion** in annual investment is needed to maintain existing services in developing countries; **USD 18 billion** is needed to increase access to improved water supply. - Agriculture accounts for **70%** of global water use; policy to exploit "win-win" solutions and manage trade-offs between water, agriculture and other sectors, including water-allocation mechanisms (OECD, 2015d), is necessary.
Sustainable cost recovery can help meet water infrastructure needs	**Innovative approaches to urban water management can enhance water security and services at the least economic, social and environmental cost.** Examples include using permeable surfaces to limit rainwater run-off and facilitate aquifer recharge or urban-rural partnerships to protect catchment areas from pollution.

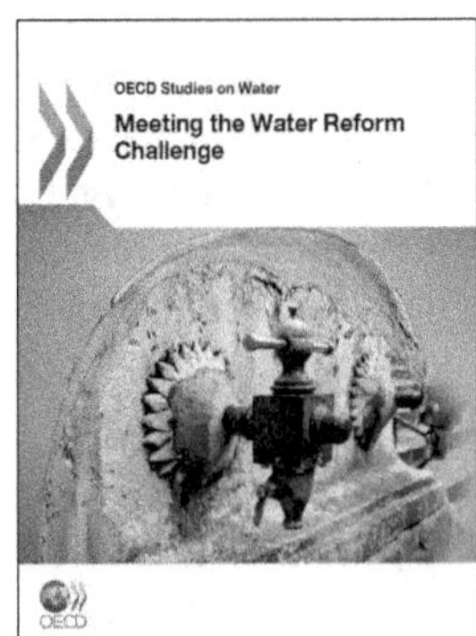

BIODIVERSITY AND ECOSYSTEMS

2011 advice	Development in advice since 2011
Sustainably manage land and soil resources to help preserve ecosystem functions and reconcile competing demands by integrating land use and territorial planning, appropriate governance and integrating biodiversity concerns into economic and sectoral policies, in addition to implementing relevant policy instruments (e.g. protected area networks, ownership rights)	**Biodiversity loss and degradation are projected to continue under current policies**, driven by land-use change and management, commercial forestry, infrastructure development, habitat encroachment, and fragmentation, pollution and climate change (OECD, 2012d). - **10%** projected global decline in biodiversity over 2010-50 **More ambitious and effective policy instruments for biodiversity, including those that generate finance and engage the private sector, are fundamental to help ensure conservation and sustainable use.** Environmental fiscal reform, payments for ecosystem services, biodiversity offsets and markets for green products contribute to achieving these goals (OECD, 2013f; OECD, forthcoming d). The appropriate choice of instrument should reflect the nature of the environmental problem and the drivers of loss. Accomplishments to date include: - **USD 6 billion** generated annually from 5 national PES programmes alone; more than 300 PES programmes implemented globally - **USD 2.4-4 billion** mobilised through biodiversity offset programmes in 2011; more than **90** offset programmes worldwide as of 2013.
Guard against biodiversity loss by strengthening conservation of habitats and species, eliminating illegal exploitation and trade, and fostering more sustainable use by integrating biodiversity concerns into economic and sectoral policies and raising public awareness, in addition to implementing relevant policy instruments (e.g. taxes, fees and charges; payment for ecosystem services [PES]; individually transferable quotas for fisheries, etc).	**Further progress on biodiversity data, metrics and indicators, including economic valuation of biodiversity and ecosystems,** is essential for more informed and efficient decision-making; National Ecosystem Assessments have an important role to play (Wilson et al., 2014) and are increasingly being developed.

2. IMPLEMENT GREEN GROWTH POLICY FRAMEWORKS
RESOURCE PRODUCTIVITY AND WASTE

Gear issue- and sector-specific policy for green growth

2011 advice	Development in advice since 2011
Drive resource productivity and sustainable materials management through integrated lifecycle-based waste, materials and product policies that internalise the cost of waste management and stimulate technological change **Improve data** on waste generation and disposal to ensure appropriate monitoring of waste flows and management	**OECD countries are becoming more resource-efficient and better at reducing waste, but increased material use in emerging economies and substitution of domestic production by imports in OECD countries are driving up global material consumption, in line with world GDP. OECD advice continues to emphasise integrated and coherent policies addressing different stages of the resource lifecycle**, including deposit-refund, upstream combined taxes and subsidies, and take-back requirements (OECD, 2015e). The results to date are as follows: • **30%** increase in GDP per material input in OECD countries since 2000; **4%** reduction in municipal waste (OECD, 2014d; OECD, 2015e); up to **80%** recycling rates for some important materials • **60%** greater levels of per capita consumption in OECD countries than the world average; **30%** estimated scope to reduce material consumption (TNO, 2013).

CLIMATE CHANGE

2011 advice	Development in advice since 2011
Climate change represents a systemic risk to growth - in addition to policy to mitigate climate change, action is required to help adapt and limit damage (e.g. by reflecting climate change risks in infrastructure design, location and material choice)	**There is uncertainty about where, when and how climate events will affect economic, social and environmental systems – and subsequent uncertainty about the resources and capacity required in the present to reduce future risks –** but the economic and social costs of increased intensity and frequency of weather-related extreme events are growing (OECD, forthcoming e). Examples of extreme events are as follows: • **AUD 4 billion** in damages, 473 deaths from 2009 heat wave in Victoria, Australia and related Black Saturday Bushfires • **USD 125 billion** in economic damages from Hurricane Katrina (2005) and USD 50 billion from Hurricane Sandy (2012) in the United States • **7-metre** potential global sea level increase from collapse of the Greenland ice sheet. **Governments are developing strategies to reduce vulnerability and exposure to climate variability; financial resources** (OECD, forthcoming e) **and better information** (Mullan et al., 2013) **are needed to drive implementation** (i.e. greater clarity around the extent of climate change and measures to monitor and evaluate adaptation strategies). • **29** OECD countries have published or planned adaptation strategies. **Effective financing includes both investment to reduce climate change-associated risks and measures to improve residual risk management;** developing ex ante financing strategies to manage impacts, improving the availability of data relevant to adaptation financing (e.g. budgetary impacts of adaptation, private-sector investment levels) and insurance reform are relevant measures.

2. IMPLEMENT GREEN GROWTH POLICY FRAMEWORKS DEVELOPMENT CO-OPERATION

Gear issue- and sector-specific policy for green growth

2011 advice	Development in advice since 2011
■ **Gear Official Development Assistance to play a role in enabling conditions for green growth** by supporting essential and resilient water and transportation infrastructure in addition to human and institutional capacity building	■ **It will be essential for developing countries to shift to green growth to achieve long-term prosperity.** Priorities for developing economies are likely to consist in managing natural resources sustainably, reducing pollution and adapting to climate change. · A national-level agenda for action on green growth is based on: 1) leadership – set a vision and integrating green growth into planning and budgetary processes; 2) policy – design and reform policies to value natural assets and align with green growth; and 3) governance – develop the capacity and resources required for implementation, monitoring and enforcement (OECD, 2013g).
■ **Match green growth and poverty objectives** in emerging and developing countries ■ **For developed and emerging countries, take into account how green growth policies may affect developing countries**	■ **Developing countries can encourage foreign direct investment by creating a favourable investment climate** through establishing regulatory and legal capacity for managing inflows, promoting and facilitating investment, attracting private investment in infrastructure, strengthening links between investment and trade, and promoting responsible business conduct (OECD, 2014e). Achievements so far are as follows: · **USD 31 billion a year,** or 24% of total bilateral Official Development Assistance targeting the global and local environment as either a principal or significant objective over 2010-12 (OECD, 2014f). · **150% increase** between 2007-09 and 2010-12 in climate-related Official Development Assistance (ODA), representing 16% of total bilateral ODA, or USD 21 billion a year.

GREEN CITIES AND REGIONS

2011 advice	Development in advice since 2011
■ **Increase urban density and use congestion charges** to help reduce energy and resource use without reducing economic growth and meet emissions reduction targets	■ **Factors beyond urban form may matter more to a city's environmental footprint than urban density; governments should focus on reforming policies that encourage excessive spatial expansion of cities and providing public transport when expansion is necessary.** In many emerging economies, large, extremely dense cities could potentially benefit from lower densities that would improve environmental and economic efficiencies and enhance well-being; strict urban-containment policies can also entail high economic and social costs (e.g. high housing prices) (OECD, 2012e).
■ **Co-ordinate policy and governance across levels of government to help drive green growth** (i.e. interaction of national sectoral policies with urban initiatives; multilevel governance to guide investment and innovation in areas like water)	■ **National and subnational policies are central to green growth in cities and must be aligned with city-level policies; in turn, urban policy can have a significant impact on greening national growth.** While senior levels of government largely define city responsibilities, resources and recourse to financial instruments, it is essential to leave scope for location-specific adaptations; engagement of local actors can also help ease stakeholder acceptance (OECD, 2013h; OECD, 2012f).

2. IMPLEMENT GREEN GROWTH POLICY FRAMEWORKS
FISHERIES

Gear issue- and sector-specific policy for green growth

2011 advice	Development in advice since 2011
Guard against over-exploitation of fish stocks through co-ordinated global action	**Stock management is the cornerstone of fisheries sustainability,** together with managing eco-system quality (biodiversity, habitat, and pollution), mitigating spillover impacts from other users and ensuring policy coherence (OECD, 2015f). - **13% more fish and an additional USD 50 billion more a year in profits** could be realised if depleted stocks were recovered and efficiently managed. **To maintain aquaculture growth in the face of environmental, spatial and legal limits,** use national development plans, institutional innovation, certification and spatial planning, as well as market-based approaches to ensure expansion is attractive to investment. - **1/3** growth potential could be realised over the next 10 years if barriers to growth, including from environmental impacts, are addressed.

OCEANS

2011 advice	Development in advice since 2011
No specific advice on ocean policy	**Emerging ocean industries, such as deep-sea oil and gas exploration, sea-bed mining and off-shore aquaculture, will have important environmental and economic implications. Further work is required** on fostering growth of ocean-based industries while better protecting the ocean environment from environmental degradation and over-exploitation of marine resources (www.oecd.org/futures/oceaneconomy.htm).

MINING

2011 advice	Development in advice since 2011
No specific advice on mining policy	**For resource-rich countries, consider including natural resource taxation as part of green growth policy packages** - If well designed, resource-rent taxation has fewer distortionary effects than many other taxes; it also enables society at large to benefit from the extraction of a country's natural resources, particularly when commodity prices are high (forthcoming OECD work).

3. ADDRESS THE SOCIAL IMPLICATIONS OF GREEN GROWTH

Labour market and skills policies to transition workers across sectors

2011 advice	Development in advice since 2011
■ **Green growth is unlikely to induce a sharp increase in jobs or labour market churn,** but will alter the sectoral composition of production and employment as green jobs are created and polluting industries shed jobs ■ **Implement active labour market and skills policies** to help manage structural adjustments to labour markets, minimise skills bottlenecks and help workers move from contracting to expanding sectors	■ **No further advice on labour market policy design for green growth beyond that developed for 2011 Green Growth Strategy (OECD, 2012g).** ■ **The number of uniquely green skills is limited, but government direction-setting and co-ordination will be required (i.e. through green growth policy frameworks) to match stimulation of green skill demand and skill development to meet that demand.** • Policy should focus on upgrading skill sets in industries experiencing minor adjustments, retraining and realigning skills in declining sectors, and preparing educational institutions and firms to support required skill adjustments for emerging occupations and sectors. Targeted support may be required for green skill development in small and medium-sized enterprises (OECD/Cedefop, 2014). ■ **Green growth has a strong local dimension, as both polluting and eco-innovative industries tend to be located in certain regions; local actors will be important to the skills transition.** Disaggregated data on jobs and skills at local level can support evidence-based policy (OECD, 2014g).

Compensation to address impacts on lower-income households

2011 advice	Development in advice since 2011
■ **Address any regressive effects of reform** through well targeted compensation programmes, taking into account the entire tax and transfer system	■ **Evidence of distributional effects of energy taxes is surprisingly scarce, given that concern about regressive impacts (i.e. disproportional impacts of reform on poorer households) seems to be a major obstacle to reform. New evidence based on experience in 21 OECD countries shows that the distributional effects of energy taxes differ by energy carrier.** Taxes on transport fuels are not regressive on average; taxes on heating fuels are slightly regressive; taxes on electricity are more regressive than taxes on heating fuels (forthcoming OECD work). ■ **Recent work on potential distributional consequences of a gradual phasing-out of all energy consumption subsides in Indonesia shows that, while in absolute terms middle and high-income households receive a great proportion of subsidies, their their phase-out would negatively impact low-income households.** Of three stylised income redistribution schemes considered to offset negative impacts, direct payment on a per household basis performed best in terms of GDP gains (forthcoming OECD work): • **0.7% GDP gains** would be achieved in 2020 if Indonesia were to remove its fossil-fuel and electricity consumption subsidies, with a direct payment-per household redistribution scheme, and • **0.8-1-6% aggregate welfare** gains would be achieved for consumers – both due to more efficient allocation of resources across sectors.

Multilateral co-ordination to address firm competitiveness concerns

2011 advice	Development in advice since 2011
■ **Address firm concerns regarding potential competitiveness impacts:** enhance understanding of how the economy is likely to adjust to new environmental regulation, to help assess potential competitiveness impacts; consider whether	■ **Competitiveness impacts of environmental reform appear to be largely overstated by industry.** Increasing the stringency of environmental policies does not harm aggregate productivity levels of manufacturing industries; rather, it is associated with a short-term increase in industry-level productivity growth (Albrizio, Koźluk and Zipperer, 2014). **Less productive firms may experience a temporary fall in growth, but gains in the most productive firms more than counter this effect.** Furthermore, stringent environmental regulations have been shown to be positively and significantly associated with higher exports of environmental goods (Sauvage, 2014). ■ Stringent environmental policies can be implemented with minimum barriers to entry and competition, according to a new indicator of Burdens on the Economy due to Environmental Policies (Koźluk, 2014).

3. ADDRESS THE SOCIAL IMPLICATIONS OF GREEN GROWTH

Multilateral co-ordination to address firm competitiveness concerns

2011 advice	Development in advice since 2011
multilateral policy co-ordination is required to address any potential "pollution haven" effects	· Policy design matters: flexible, market-based instruments such as taxes and trading schemes are friendlier to productivity growth. ▪ **Ex post evaluation of the competitiveness impacts of environmental measures is one tool to assess potential detrimental effects on firm output or employment, but is currently underutilised** owing to lack of access to micro-level data allowing for comparison between firms (Arlinghaus 2015). ▪ **One ex post analysis of the impact of a German electricity tax implemented in 1999 on firms in the manufacturing sector shows no deterioration in their competitiveness of firms** subject to the full tax rate relative to firms subject to a reduced rate (forthcoming OECD work).

4. MONITOR PROGRESS

2011 advice	Development in advice since 2011
▪ **Develop indicators to track progress, across:** · the transition to a low-carbon, resource-efficient economy · preserving the natural asset base · the environmental dimension of quality of life · implementing policies for green growth, while realising its economic opportunities	▪ **Stronger, sustained efforts are needed to improve the efficient use of energy and natural resources** to reverse environmental damage, maintain the economy's natural asset base and improve people's quality of life (OECD, 2014a). · **Since 1990,** the environmental productivity of OECD economies in terms of carbon, energy and materials has grown, but with wide variations across countries and sectors. OECD countries now generate more economic value per unit of material resources; efforts to recycle waste are starting to pay off; and nutrient use in agriculture is improving, with surpluses declining relative to production. · **In many areas, productivity gains are small and environmental pressures remain high.** Carbon emissions continue to rise; fossil fuels continue to dominate the energy mix, sometimes benefiting from government support; the consumption of material resources to support economic growth remains high; and many valuable materials continue to be disposed of as waste. ▪ **A representative set of "headline" indicators can help crystallise and track central concepts of green growth,** and enhance understanding by policy makers and the general public. (https://stats.oecd.org/Index.aspx?DataSetCode=GREEN_GROWTH). · **The 6 headline indicators are:** carbon productivity; material productivity; environmentally adjusted, whole-of-economy (multifactor) productivity; natural resource indices; changes in land use and cover; and population exposure to air pollution. ▪ **The combination of economic and environmental data is challenging owing to differences in classification, terminology and timeframes.** The System of Environmental-Economic Accounting (SEEA) – a global statistical standard bridging economic and environmental data – is a useful tool to help develop green growth indicators. · **12 countries and 3 institutions** comprise the OECD Task Force on implementation of the SEEA established in 2013 to support development of the headline indicators. · **4 background notes** have been completed to date, relating to compilation of air emission and natural resource accounts, compilationcompilation of natural-resource in physical units and valuation of natural-resource stocks. ▪ **Green growth indicator development requires progress on two fronts: methodological advancement and addressing data gaps as well as data quality issues.** The risk is that the lack of quality country-level data will hamper indicator production and use in country surveillance and policy analysis.

UPDATING THE GREEN GROWTH STRATEGY

The work undertaken since 2011 and the country experience outlined in Chapter 2 suggest five areas of adjustment to the Green Growth Strategy:

- Greater emphasis should be placed on enhancing understanding of longer-term complementarities and trade-offs between economic and environmental goals, including through more effective use of cost-benefit analysis, to better integrate environmental priorities into structural economic policies.
- Policy should focus more sharply on enhancing public understanding and trust in green growth reform by paying more attention to policies' distributional implications as an integral part of green growth policy design (i.e. and not as a secondary step to policy implementation).
- Increased efforts should be made to ensure policy alignment both within and across sectors to support green growth and prevent policy incoherence or misalignments frustrating reform.
- The ocean economy and mining should be integrated into the Strategy as issue-specific policy areas to be geared to green growth.
- Green growth headline indicators should be used to raise awareness, measure progress and identify opportunities and risks.

The five updates to the Green Growth Strategy are marked in green in Figure 3.1 and addressed in turn below. Important work has also emerged on the particular set of challenges and opportunities green growth represents for developing and emerging economies. The 2011 Green Growth Strategy addressed the implementation of green growth in developing countries, but the work since 2011 suggests that further emphasis is merited in this area. Accordingly, green growth in developing countries is also addressed below.

Update No. 1: Enhance understanding of complementarities and trade-offs between economic and environmental goals, to better integrate environmental priorities into structural economic reform priorities

Advance understanding of the economic opportunities and challenges of environmental policy, and economic and well-being costs of environmental degradation, to inform green growth objective-setting. To implement green growth, governments must bind together environmental and structural economic reform priorities in a single, coherent agenda. Important work has been undertaken since the 2011 Green Growth Strategy to try to help governments gauge the impact of environmental regulation on growth, as well as the potential feedbacks of environmental degradation on economic growth and well-being. These issues are fundamental to setting priorities for green growth and helping governments articulate how economic and environmental priorities align. The work underscores the importance of accelerating understanding of the interplay between economic and environmental goals.

How – if at all – does environmental regulation impact economic growth?

Measure stringency of environmental policy and its impact on growth. A threshold issue in determining the economic effects of environmental policies is determining how to evaluate the costs imposed by policy on polluting and other environmentally harmful activity in a way that enables comparison across countries and time. The challenge is to reflect the quantitative and qualitative information contained in laws and regulations in a comparable measure of stringency. A newly developed OECD indicator – the Environmental Policy Stringency Indicator – addresses this issue (Botta and Koźluk, 2014). It demonstrates that environmental policies in OECD countries have become significantly more stringent over the past two decades and enables assessing the impacts of this tightened policy on n growth.

Environmental policy tightening since 1990 has had no negative effect on OECD country productivity growth.

FIGURE 3.1 – THREE STEPS TO GREEN GROWTH: THE GREEN GROWTH STRATEGY IN 2015

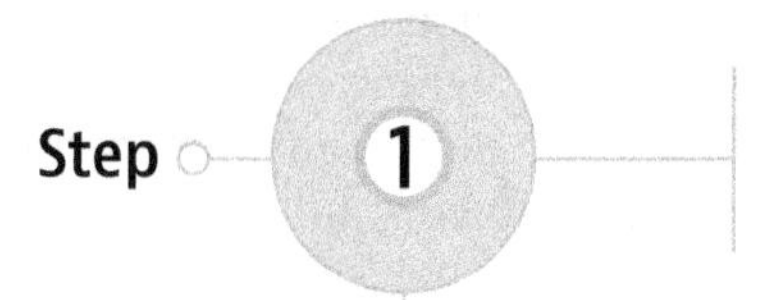

ALIGN GROWTH AND ENVIRONMENTAL OBJECTIVES

Gear core economic policies to mutually reinforce growth and conservation of natural capital.

- ENHANCE UNDERSTANDING OF COMPLEMENTARITIES AND TRADE-OFFS BETWEEN ECONOMIC AND ENVIRONMENTAL GOALS.
- Link environmental objectives with economic reform policies, prioritising more effective use of cost-benefit analysis.
- Anchor green growth in core economic ministries; drive cross-portfolio co-ordination.
- Address constraints to green investment and innovation.

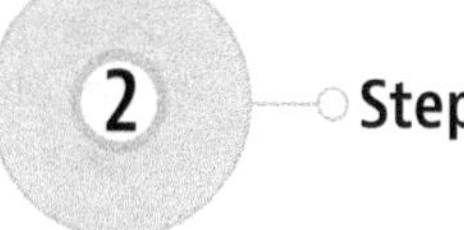

IMPLEMENT GREEN GROWTH POLICY FRAMEWORKS

Develop policy packages to price pollution and provide incentives for efficient resource use, PRIORITISING MORE EFFECTIVE USE OF COST-BENEFIT ANALYSIS.

- Pricing instruments to drive broad-based, least cost action (tradable permit systems, taxes).
- Regulation to provide incentives for green growth (emissions performance standards, energy efficiency).
- Subsidies to promote green technologies, products and practices; fossil fuel subsidy reform.
- Information measures to guide consumer behaviour.

Gear sectoral policies for green growth, ENSURING POLICY ALIGNMENT BOTH WITHIN AND ACROSS SECTORS;

- INVESTMENT AND FINANCE | INNOVATION
- TAXATION | TRADE AND FOREIGN DIRECT INVESTMENT
- ENERGY | TRANSPORT | AGRICULTURE
- WATER | BIODIVERSITY AND ECOSYSTEMS
- WASTE | CLIMATE CHANGE
- DEVELOPMENT | GREEN CITIES AND REGIONS
- FISHERIES
- + MINING | + OCEANS

ADDRESS THE SOCIAL IMPLICATIONS OF GREEN GROWTH (Previously Step 3)

Address distributional impacts to facilitate reform and promote inclusiveness.

- Labour market and skills policies to transition workers across sectors.
- Compensation to address impacts on lower-income households.
- Multilateral coordination to address firm competitiveness concerns.

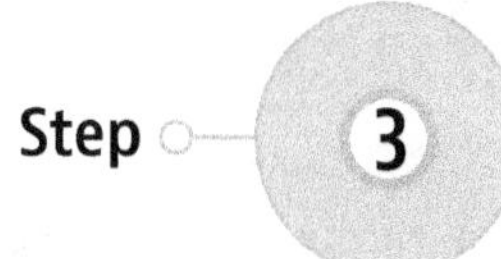

MONITOR PROGRESS

Develop indicators to track progress, INCLUDING SECTOR-SPECIFIC INDICATORS; GATHER DATA TO SUPPORT NEW INDICATORS; USE HEADLINE INDICATORS TO ADVANCE CENTRAL ELEMENTS OF GREEN GROWTH.

- Transition to a low-carbon, resource efficient economy.
- Preservation of the natural asset base.
- Environmental quality of life.
- Economic opportunities and effective policy.

Environmental policy tightening since 1990 has had no negative effect on productivity growth in OECD countries (Albrizio, Koźluk and Zipperer, 2014). In fact, empirical evidence of the impacts of environmental policy stringency on productivity growth shows that tightening policies results in a temporary increase in productivity growth, and thus an overall increase in manufacturing industries' production efficiency. Less productive firms experience a temporary fall in growth – potentially needing higher investments to comply with new regulation – but the gains experienced by the most productive firms more than counter this effect – e.g. by seizing new market opportunities and deploying new technologies.

More stringent environmental regulation can also lead to economic opportunities (Sauvage, 2014). The Environmental Policy Stringency Indicator has been used to examine the relationship between environmental regulation stringency and country exports of environmental goods. Stringent environmental regulation positively affects countries' specialisation in environmental products, even in sectors such as solid-waste management or wastewater treatment.

An ex post, micro-level study of a German electricity tax applied to manufacturing sectors firms in 1999 supports the finding that environmental policy is likely to have little impact on manufacturing industry productivity.[1] Firms subject to the full tax rate suffered no deterioration in competitiveness relative to otherwise similar firms that faced reduced rates. This result is particularly significant because the applied reduction amounted to up to EUR 31.6 per tonne of carbon dioxide (CO_2) when measured as an effective tax rate on the carbon content in the average unit of electricity. Few additional ex post assessments of competitiveness impacts of environmental policy are available, because a lack of micro-data frustrates effective comparison among firms (Arlinghaus, 2015). The few that exist support the finding that no significant aggregate negative effects result from environmental policy implementation.[2]

The newly developed Burdens on the Economy due to Environmental Policies (BEEP) indicator suggests that stringent environmental policies can be implemented with minimum barriers to entry and competition (Koźluk, 2014). Barriers to entry and competition stemming from environmental policy differs across countries, but are not correlated with the environmental policies' stringency; rather, they depend on policy design. While trade-offs may be unavoidable in some cases, adequate design of environmental policies can help minimise adverse effects on competition. Market-based instruments, such as taxes and trading schemes, tend to have a more robust positive effect on productivity growth. Administrative procedures, advantages conferred through policy to existing firms and policy that is non-neutral with respect to technological choices can also affect competition and entry.

The bottom-line message for governments is that, subject to good policy design, more stringent environmental policies can be implemented without productivity loss at the macroeconomic or industry levels. Further work on the effects of environmental policy on investment, firm entry-exit, and international trade and relocation, as well as a greater comprehension of investment, employment and production processes, would enhance understanding of environmental policies' broader economic effects. Refinements are also planned to the Environmental Policy Stringency Indicator to expand policy instrument, sector and country coverage. Further ex post work at the micro-level would also help advance understanding of the consequences of environmental policies. Where concerns relating to the competitiveness impacts of environmental policies persist, adjustments to policy design or greater harmonisation across countries may be warranted.

What sorts of feedbacks is environmental degradation likely to have on the economy?

Environmental degradation can have substantial negative feedbacks on GDP and well-being owing, for example, to poorer health, water shortages, land degradation or extreme weather events.

1.0-3.3% global GDP losses from selected aspects of climate change by 2060.

Quantifying the economic impacts of environmental damage. Global GDP losses resulting from selected aspects of climate change alone are projected to reach between 1.0-3.3% by 2060, principally due to lower agricultural productivity and rising sea levels. These figures do not include the effect of changes in extreme weather events, water stress and large-scale disruptions. The global figure masks much more significant (Dellink et al., 2014) impacts on specific sectors and regions.

Furthermore, it does not include estimated losses from rising health costs and productivity losses related to air pollution, water scarcity or land degradation – nor does it include the effects of biodiversity loss, climate change-induced extreme weather events or potentially irreversible large-scale disruptions to the climate system. All have scope to be extremely costly.

For example, the economic cost of outdoor air pollution, in terms of the value of lives lost and ill health, is much higher than previously thought (OECD, 2014b. (OECD, 2014b). The average cost of air pollution-related deaths and illnesses amounted to 4% of GDP in OECD countries on average in 2010 (around half of it due to pollution from road transport) and over 10% of GDP in some OECD countries (e.g. Hungary). Still in 2010, air pollution-related deaths and illnesses cost the equivalent of 12% of GDP in China in 2010, while they amounted to 9% of GDP in India in 2005.

4% of GDP, average cost of air pollution-related deaths and illnesses in OECD countries, 2010.

Analysis of the feedback loop from rising environmental impacts to GDP and other dimensions of well-being is still at an early stage. More work is needed to assess the economic consequences of risks posed by climate change at the regional and sectoral level, and to quantify the feedbacks of air pollution and the link between land, water and energy. The possibility of quantifying water-economy linkages, as well as impacts of resource scarcity and loss of biodiversity and ecosystem services, needs to be assessed. Work is also ongoing to better understand the economic costs of the health impacts caused by outdoor air pollution.

The work underscores that governments should integrate longer-term perspectives that factor in interactions between the environment and the economy when developing policy tools. Analytical frameworks considering likely long-term changes in underlying economic structures can be adjusted to reflect the economic damages from climate change, which apply significant pressure on global output and living conditions in the long run. For example, as part of the project OECD@100, aiming to devise scenarios for the global economy at the 2060 horizon, the ENV-Linkages model is used to generate predictions on greenhouse gas emissions, consistent with the long-term growth and trade scenarios.

Prioritise more effective use of cost-benefit analysis to guide policy choices

There is much scope to improve ex ante and ex post assessments of policy proposals, as well as investment projects, by making better use of cost-benefit analysis, including economic valuation of environmental externalities.[3] Government policy decisions and investment proposals can have large environmental impacts, which should be methodically taken into account in ex ante and ex post policy and project assessments. Yet clear guidelines for using cost-benefit analysis are virtually non-existent across countries for ex post policy and project assessments, and exist in only few countries for general ex ante policy assessments. They do, however, exist in a number of countries to evaluate energy and transport investment. Much more effective use of cost-benefit analysis is essential to help inform policy decisions from an environmental perspective, and further guidance on the subject is due for release in 2016.

Assessments where mortality impacts are significant should include "values of statistical lives", ideally based on national willingness-to-pay surveys (i.e. how much individuals are willing to pay to secure a marginal reduction in premature death risk) (OECD, 2012a). Work is ongoing to develop a standard by which to measure the cost of morbidities.

Update No. 2: Enhance public trust in green growth by addressing the social impacts of reform in OECD countries as well as developing and emerging economies

Green growth reform is likely to encounter political opposition if policy reforms do not take careful account of any social impacts of reform. Social objectives should be considered and pursued jointly with green growth objectives. The potential distributional impacts of green growth merit greater policy focus, both because green growth policy should not exacerbate inequality – already on the rise in many countries – and because reform depends on effectively addressing the political challenges associated with the transition. Country experience with carbon pricing – as addressed in Chapter 2 – demonstrates the point. Some governments may need to consider pursuing more actively policy mechanisms other than direct pricing, such as implicit pricing and regulation.

Green growth is a labour and social policy issue, too. The potential social implications of green growth reform should be addressed ex ante, as a fundamental part of policy design, rather than as an afterthought to policy implementation. To deliver short-term benefits to the populations most vulnerable to proposed changes, policies will need to be designed to share fairly the economic and welfare benefits of green growth. Thus, Step 2 of the revised Green Growth Strategy integrates addressing social impacts, to be considered as an integral part of developing green growth policy frameworks. Addressing the social impacts of green growth was a discrete step in the 2011 Green Growth Strategy (previously Step 3).

Public trust is a central pillar for reform: governments must nurture it.

In addition to the competitiveness impacts discussed in Update 1 above, the potential labour market and household impacts of green growth are also relevant, and work needs to advance in this area. The 2014 Green Growth and Sustainable Development (GGSD) Forum – which focused on the social impacts of green growth in 2014 – identified considerable scope to advance work on labour and household issues.[4] The Green Growth Knowledge Platform, launched by the OECD in January 2012 in conjunction with the Global Green Growth Institute,[5] the United Nations Environment Programme[6] and the World Bank[7] to help identify and address major knowledge gaps in green growth theory and practices,[8] is initiating a Research Committee on Inclusiveness to advance work in this area.

The green transition is unlikely to have a big impact on overall employment, but good framework policies are required to smooth shifts in the sectoral composition of employment. While no "treasure trove" of new jobs is likely to result, there is scope for potentially large shifts in labour demand in certain industries – e.g. in the energy sector – and significant local jobs impacts, both positive and negative. Widespread – but mostly incremental – changes will also occur in skill requirements across the economy. The resulting income effects raise the question of equitable distribution of gains and losses. Supporting the transition will require more accurate projections of the likely structural changes and potential labour market reactions at the country level. It will also require a better understanding of green growth's impact on skill patterns and demand, as well as more modelling on the impacts on relative pay associated with particular skills. Filling these gaps, and other gaps in existing knowledge, can help ensure that the growth and employment potential of the transition is fully exploited.[9]

Further work should be undertaken on the distributional impact of green growth policies, with a focus on better understanding the significance of environmental policy's regressive effects on households. Green growth policy-related price increases (for example, potential electricity price increases) could disproportionally impact on lower-income households because any incremental price adjustments are likely to represent a larger share of their budgets. Further analysis on energy taxes' impact on energy affordability at the household level would be useful in that context. Absolute measures of energy affordability, as well as possible energy tax reforms, could be examined.

Such analysis requires rich data sets, which are essential to understanding household behaviour by integrating information on the distributional impacts of reform with information on the incidence and intensity of poverty. Analysis should focus on determining whether best practices emerge from experience to date (including from a political feasibility perspective) and how best to address barriers to environmental tax reform, given its potential for revenue recycling.[10]

To address some of these gaps, the OECD is contemplating cross-committee work to enhance modelling capabilities with a view to assessing labour market consequences for different kinds of workers and better model the effects on households at different stages of income distribution. Case study analysis on specific policies, and their impact at local and city levels, would also help inform policy.

Update No. 3: Ensure that policies with the potential to affect green growth are coherent and aligned within and across sectors

Gearing sectoral and issue-specific policy to supporting green growth means aligning policies across sectors, as well as ensuring policies within specific areas are internally coherent and oriented towards green growth. Recent work reiterates the need for governments to look across policies both within and between sectors when implementing green growth policy frameworks. Well-designed structural reforms can also help drive green growth.

Several misalignments in existing policy frameworks currently hinder the transition to green growth. For example, from a climate policy perspective these misalignments exist in core, cross-cutting economic policy domains – e.g. investment, taxation, innovation and international trade – as well as policy governing specific areas that are fundamental to this transition – e.g. electricity systems, urban mobility and rural land use. Since almost all economic activities generate greenhouse gas emissions, climate policy interacts with policies in many more areas. Climate change policy instruments, and the economic signals they create, overlay and interact with the goals and instruments of existing policy frameworks. The result can be frictions, unintended consequences, or even actively conflicting policy objectives. Where policies relating to international trade are concerned, for example, three policy areas were examined: trade liberalisation; domestic subsidies and their impact on global value chains for renewable energy; and the machinery of trade itself, i.e. international maritime and aviation transport. Misalignments identified include, for example, policies that support domestic renewable energy industries, but are restrictive of international trade and therefore act to push up costs for domestic and international firms alike.

Misalignments in government policy are acting as a major break on reform.

Aligning Policies for the Transition to a Low-carbon Economy (OECD, forthcoming a) offers a new approach to facilitating the implementation and improving the effectiveness of climate action, with the first broad diagnosis of misalignments between overall policy, regulatory frameworks and climate goals. It identifies a number of opportunities for realigning policies to enable an efficient and cost-effective shift to a low-carbon economy. Addressing these misalignments offers an opportunity for governments – including ministries not yet sufficiently mobilised in developing and implementing climate-response strategies – to take a comprehensive look across policy frameworks and start improving their coherence. Solving a policy misalignment with climate goals will often facilitate the achievement of other policy objectives; it can make climate policy more acceptable to various stakeholders and climate objectives more achievable.

Recent work on government taxation of energy use drives home the need for governments to assess existing sectoral policy to ensure it is geared to reform, and remove any barriers or distortions (OECD, 2013b). The structure and level of current energy taxation policy in many countries is not coherent from an environmental perspective, despite its considerable impact on energy prices, energy usage and the environment. In many cases, variations in tax rates across energy forms, uses and users of energy are not clearly motivated and do not reflect associated environmental costs. The example of differences in the tax treatment of gasoline and diesel for road use – 33 of the 34 OECD countries tax diesel at lower rates than gasoline, despite greater environmental and social externalities (Harding, 2014a) –is discussed in Chapter 3. In the electricity sector, coal is often taxed at a lower rate than natural gas, biofuels or waste; taxes on electricity consumption also provide no signals about the different environmental impacts of the primary energy sources generating electricity. Given that taxes on energy products amount to 72% of all revenues from environmentally related taxation in OECD countries (Harding, 2014a), governments should urgently reappraise whether energy tax settings are suited to environmental and social goals.

Update No. 4: Consider the ocean economy and mining in gearing sectoral policies for green growth

The ocean economy has had limited attention as a green growth issue to date. Yet emerging ocean industries – which include offshore wind, tidal and wave energy; offshore oil and gas extraction in deep-sea and other extreme locations (e.g. the Arctic); sea-bed mining; marine aquaculture; marine biotechnology; and ocean-related tourism and leisure – have important economic and environmental implications, including growth, employment and innovation prospects. The ocean is already under stress from over-exploitation, pollution, declining biodiversity and climate change. Realising the full potential of emerging ocean industries requires further focusing on responsible, sustainable approaches to developing the ocean's economic potential. Work is being undertaken to help governments assess emerging ocean industries' potential contribution to green growth and boost their long-term prospects, while managing environmental and ocean ecosystems impacts such as ocean acidification.[11] Forthcoming work will also assess "green innovation" in the maritime transport sector.

Mining is another area that was not explicitly covered in the 2011 Green Growth Strategy. Resource-rich countries should consider and provide for the environmental impacts of resource extraction when designing green growth strategies. For example, recent work demonstrates the potential to make better use of natural-resource taxation in green growth policy packages. If well-designed, resource-rent taxation in resource-rich countries has fewer distortionary effects on the economy than many other taxes. It also represents a "fair" tax, which enables society at large to benefit from a country's natural-resource extraction and potentially allows reducing other more distortionary taxes. Further work is planned for 2015-16 to help governments – particularly in developing countries – receive an appropriate return on the extraction of their non-renewable resources, including through assistance on resource-rent taxation where requested, in collaboration with co-operation partners such as the International Monetary Fund and the World Bank.

Update No. 5: Further develop and use headline indicators to raise awareness, measure progress and identify opportunities and risks

A smaller set of "headline" indicators complements a full set of green growth indicators by helping to articulate and monitor progress in central elements of green growth. Development of headline indicators was foreshadowed in the 2011 Green Growth Strategy. Of the six headline indicators that were proposed at that time (Figure 3.2), two – carbon productivity and non-energy material productivity – have been produced. They aim to capture the efficiency of the economy in terms of the amount of CO_2 generated from economic activity (both on a production and consumption basis) and the amount of raw materials and other commodities needed to support a certain level of economic output.

Ongoing data collection is needed to evaluate and monitor the transition towards green growth.

Methodological work to develop the other indicators is ongoing, through an OECD Task Force comprising 12 countries and 3 institutions. The indicators include environmentally adjusted, whole-economy (multifactor) productivity; a natural-resource index to monitor the sustainability of the natural asset base, including renewable and non-renewable assets; changes in land cover and use, to assess the pressures on biodiversity and ecosystems not covered by the natural-resource index; and population exposure to air pollution ($PM_{2.5}$), highlighting an important element of people's environmental quality of life. The potential of earth observation and other geospatial data to help produce the indicators related to land cover and use, as well as population exposure to air-pollution indicators, is being assessed. Finally, a headline indicator relating to the economic opportunities associated with the transition to green growth will eventually be proposed, but has not yet been identified. The development of several candidate indicators, including environment-related technological innovation, environment-related taxes, and environmental policy stringency and design, is well advanced. The headline indicators merit reflection in the Green Growth Strategy.

Advancing the green growth measurement agenda requires progress on two fronts: methodological advancement of indicators and data collection to enable their production. Governments need to continue their efforts to ensure data availability and quality to underpin the production of green growth indicators and their use in country surveillance policy analysis relevant to green growth. The role of national statistics agencies is vital. Once indicators have been developed, proxy indicators or preliminary estimates with appropriate caveats can be used to continuously improve the availability and quality of underlying data in countries where quality data is not yet available. Data gaps include internationally comparable environmental-economic accounts (including of air emissions, natural resources such as mineral and energy assets, freshwater, forests and soils). Air emission accounts are currently available only in Australia, Canada, Norway, Switzerland, Turkey and European Union Member States. Mineral and energy asset accounts, supported by data on natural-resource extraction costs, are generally only compiled by resource-rich countries – but as all countries draw on the same pool of resources, information on remaining stocks is a public good for both resource-poor and resource-rich countries. Another challenge is ensuring the availability of internationally comparable data on pollutant emissions into the environment (as currently collected nationally in Pollutant Release and Transfer Registers) or the general state of the environment (e.g. air and water quality, and biodiversity and ecosystem health, including marine environments) – which is in many ways a prerequisite for monitoring green growth progress.

FIGURE 3.2 – SIX HEADLINE INDICATORS FOR GREEN GROWTH

TRANSITION TO A RESOURCE-EFFICIENT, LOW-CARBON ECONOMY

How efficient is the use of environmental resources and services?

Carbon productivity

Non-energy material (resource) productivity

Environmentally-adjusted, whole-economy (multi-factor) productivity

ENVIRONMENTAL QUALITY OF LIFE

How are environment conditions impacting on human well-being? What kind of access does the public have to environmental services and amenities?

Population exposure to air pollution (PM 2.5) (health impacts of environmental degradation and related costs)

NATURAL ASSET BASE

Are environmental and economic resources being preserved, to support future growth?

Natural resource index

Changes in land cover and use (pressures on biodiversity and ecosystems)

ECONOMIC OPPORTUNITIES AND EFFECTIVE POLICY

How effective is current green growth policy? Are the economic opportunities associated with the transition being seized?

Headline indicator to be determined

Sectoral indicators can help advance green growth in areas such as agriculture and energy. Recent work on agricultural indicators demonstrates the value of tailoring indicators to track progress towards green growth in specific sectors. *Green Growth Indicators for Agriculture: A Preliminary Assessment* (OECD, 2014c) proposes 25 indicators to capture key aspects of a low-carbon, resource-efficient agricultural sector. The International Energy Agency's annual *Tracking Clean Energy Progress* report (IEA, 2014d) assesses progress in terms of technology penetration, market creation and technology development across all parts of the energy system, including power generation, end use, systems integration, and carbon capture and storage.

Respond to the particular set of challenges and opportunities that green growth represents for developing and emerging economies

Green growth will be essential to the long-term prosperity of developing and emerging economies, but policies will need to be designed to balance potential short-term trade-offs and respond to the specific challenges facing developing and emerging economies. *Putting Green Growth at the Heart of Development* report (OECD, 2013g) notes the challenges and policy choices in developing countries are different from those in developed countries. They stem from the large informal economy; high levels of poverty and inequality; weak capacity and resources for innovation and (both public and private) investment; an urgent need for rapid development, economic growth and welfare improvement; and few mechanisms to ensure that those who protect natural assets receive large enough financial incentives to maintain them. Thus, developing countries may require a different sequencing and mix of policy instruments than developed countries.

Green growth will be essential to the long-term prosperity of developing and emerging economies; policy must be tailored to their needs.

NEXT STEPS – ENRICHING GREEN GROWTH ADVICE

The updates proposed in this chapter suggest a number of forward work priorities for governments, the OECD and other relevant institutions. Figure 3.3 collates them, to help better target future analysis and policy advice in support of country implementation efforts. While the priorities raised below merit particular consideration from governments, they should not detract from the need to consider the full suite of measures outlined in the Green Growth Strategy in implementing reform.

FIGURE 3.3 – FORWARD WORK PRIORITIES TO ENRICH GREEN GROWTH ADVICE

Enhance understanding of complementarities and trade-offs between economic and environmental goals, to better integrate environmental priorities into structural economic reform priorities

- **Further work on the effects of environmental policy on investment, firm entry-exit, international trade and relocation, employment and production processes, to enhance understanding of broader economic effects of environmental policies.**
- Further ex-post policy evaluation studies at the micro-level to help advance understanding of the consequences of environmental policies on households and firms.
- **Further work to assess economic consequences of risks from climate change at regional and sectoral level, and to quantify feedbacks of air pollution and the link between land, water and energy.**
- Increase understanding of the economic costs of health impacts of outdoor air pollution.
- **Systematise accounting for interactions between the environment and the economy when using policy guidance tools such as multidimensional frameworks and long-term scenarios.**
- Use cost-benefit analysis routinely and systematise it in policy design and project implementation.

Enhance public trust in green growth by effectively addressing social impacts of reform, in OECD countries as well as developing and emerging economies

- **Enhance understanding of how significant regressive effects of environmental policy are likely to be on households; analyse the impact of energy taxes on the affordability of energy at the household level; examine absolute measures of energy affordability, as well as possible energy tax reforms; identify emerging best practices from experience to date including from a political-economy perspective.**
- Advance work on "second-best" policy instruments, such as implicit pricing and regulatory approaches, recognising the challenges currently associated with "first-best" direct pricing mechanisms (including likely cost increases).
- **Undertake work to develop more accurate projections of the size of likely structural changes in labour markets and potential labour-market reactions at country level.**
- Enhance understanding of likely impacts on the demand for working skills.
- **Advance modelling on impacts on relative pay associated with particular skills.**
- Advance knowledge of ways to design green growth policies so that they contribute to reducing poverty, particularly in developing and emerging economies.

Ensure that environmental policies are coherent and aligned within and across sectors

- Assess sectoral and issue-specific policy to ensure policies are internally coherent and orientated for green growth. The OECD Taxing Energy Use project provides a starting point to assess government fiscal policy.
- Assess sectoral and issue-specific policy to ensure policies are aligned across sectors to support green growth. The OECD Aligning Policies for the Transition to a Low-carbon Economy project provides a starting point with respect to climate policy.
- Consider further work to help governments align policies within and across sectors for green growth. One potential example is work to assess policy alignment for biodiversity conservation and sustainable use across sectors such as agriculture, tourism and fisheries.
- Redouble efforts to eliminate the USD 640 billion support for fossil fuels currently being spent by governments.
- Re-invigorate efforts to gear innovation systems to both accelerate innovation and direct innovation to green technologies and processes. The primary mechanism to advance this effort at the OECD will be the forthcoming 2015 Green Growth and Sustainable Development Forum, on "Enabling the next industrial revolution: Systems innovation for green growth". The process to revise the Innovation Strategy is also relevant.

Consider the ocean economy and mining in gearing sectoral policies for green growth

- Advance work to consider green growth issues related to emerging ocean industries and mining.

Use headline indicators to raise awareness, measure progress and identify opportunities and risks

- Continue to advance methodological development of the green growth headline indicators and broader green growth indicator set, including alignment with minimum barriers to entry and competition indicators.
- Continue to improve measuring of natural-capital stocks in physical and monetary terms, including measurement of land and natural resources, with a view to implementing key aspects of the System of Environmental-Economic Accounting.
- Consider developing sectoral indicators to track and monitor progress within sectors.

Factor in the particular set of challenges and opportunities green growth represents for developing and emerging economies

- Explicitly identify the inter-linkages between the OECD Green Growth Strategy and the OECD Development Strategy and advance knowledge of the different sequencing and mix of green growth policy instruments needed in developing and emerging economies.
- Incorporate environmental considerations into the economic and governance policy advice provided by the OECD to developing and emerging economies, including through relevant peer review processes, the Global Relations Strategy and OECD regional programmes.

CHAPTER REFERENCES

Albrizio, S., T. Koźluk and V. Zipperer (2014), "Empirical Evidence on the Effects of Environmental Policy Stringency on Productivity Growth", *OECD Economics Department Working Papers,* No. 1179, OECD Publishing, Paris, http://dx.doi.org/10.1787/5jxrjnb36b40-en.

Arlinghaus, J. (2015), "Impacts of Carbon Pricing on Indicators of Competitiveness: A Review of Empirical Findings", *OECD Environment Working Papers,* No. 87, OECD Publishing, Paris, http://dx.doi.org/10.1787/5js37p21grzq-en.

Bahar, H., J. Egeland and R. Steenblik (2013), "Domestic Incentive Measures for Renewable Energy with Possible Trade Implications", *OECD Trade and Environment Working Papers,* No. 2013/01, OECD Publishing, Paris, http://dx.doi.org/10.1787/5k44srlksr6f-en.

Botta, E. and T. Koźluk (2014), "Measuring Environmental Policy Stringency in OECD Countries: A Composite Index Approach", *OECD Economics Department Working Papers,* No. 1177, OECD Publishing, Paris, http://dx.doi.org/10.1787/5jxrjnc45gvg-en.

Criscuolo, C. and C. Menon (2014), "Environmental Policies and Risk Finance in the Green Sector: Cross-country Evidence", *OECD Science, Technology and Industry Working Papers,* No. 2014/01, OECD Publishing, Paris, http://dx.doi.org/10.1787/5jz6wn918j37-en.

Criscuolo, C., et al. (2014), "Renewable Energy Policies and Cross-border Investment: Evidence from Mergers and Acquisitions in Solar and Wind Energy", *OECD Science, Technology and Industry Working Papers,* No. 2014/03, OECD Publishing, Paris, http://dx.doi.org/10.1787/5jxv9f3r9623-en.

Dellink, R. et al. (2014), "Consequences of Climate Change Damages for Economic Growth: A Dynamic Quantitative Assessment", *OECD Economics Department Working Papers,* No. 1135, OECD Publishing, Paris, http://dx.doi.org/10.1787/5jz2bxb8kmf3-en.

Dechezleprêtre, A., I. Haščič and N. Johnstone (2015), "Invention and International Diffusion of Water Conservation and Availability Technologies: Evidence from Patent Data", *OECD Environment Working Papers,* No. 82, OECD Publishing, Paris, http://dx.doi.org/10.1787/5js679fvllhg-en.

Egli, F., C. Menon and N. Johnstone (forthcoming), "Quality and Breakthrough Inventions: The Case of Climate Mitigation Technologies" *OECD Science, Technology and Industry Working Papers.*

Greene, J. and N.A. Braathen (2014), "Tax Preferences for Environmental Goals: Use, Limitations and Preferred Practices", *OECD Environment Working Papers,* No. 71, OECD Publishing, Paris, http://dx.doi.org/10.1787/5jxwrr4hkd6l-en.

Harding, M. (2014a), "The Diesel Differential: Differences in the Tax Treatment of Gasoline and Diesel for Road Use", *OECD Taxation Working Papers,* No. 21, OECD Publishing, Paris, http://dx.doi.org/10.1787/5jz14cd7hk6b-en.

Harding, M. (2014b), "Personal Tax Treatment of Company Cars and Commuting Expenses: Estimating the Fiscal and Environmental Costs", *OECD Taxation Working Papers,* No. 20, OECD Publishing, Paris, http://dx.doi.org/10.1787/5jz14cg1s7vl-en.

IEA (2014a), *World Energy Outlook 2014,* IEA, Paris, http://dx.doi.org/10.1787/weo-2014-en.

IEA (2014b), *Energy Technology Perspectives 2014,* IEA, Paris, http://dx.doi.org/10.1787/energy_tech-2014-en.

IEA (2014c), *Medium-Term Renewable Energy Market Report 2014,* IEA, Paris, http://dx.doi.org/10.1787/renewmar-2014-en.

IEA (2014d), *Tracking Clean Energy Progress Report 2014,* IEA, Paris, http://www.iea.org/etp/tracking/.

Kaminker, C. et al. (2013), "Institutional Investors and Green Infrastructure Investments: Selected Case Studies", *OECD Working Papers on Finance, Insurance and Private Pensions,* No. 35, OECD Publishing, Paris, http://dx.doi.org/10.1787/5k3xr8k6jb0n-en.

Kennedy, C. and J. Corfee-Morlot (2013), "Past performance and future needs for low carbon climate resilient infrastructure – An investment perspective", www.sciencedirect.com/science/article/pii/S0301421513002814.

Koźluk, T. (2014), "The Indicators of the Economic Burdens of Environmental Policy Design: Results from the OECD Questionnaire", *OECD Economics Department Working Papers,* No. 1178, OECD Publishing, Paris, http://dx.doi.org/10.1787/5jxrjnbnbm8v-en.

Mullan, M. et al. (2013), "National Adaptation Planning: Lessons from OECD Countries", *OECD Environment Working Papers,* No. 54, OECD Publishing, Paris, http://dx.doi.org/10.1787/5k483jpfpsq1-en.

OECD/Cedefop (2014), *Greener Skills and Jobs, OECD Green Growth Studies,* OECD Publishing, Paris, http://dx.doi.org/10.1787/9789264208704-en.

OECD/ITF (2015), *ITF Transport Outlook 2015,* OECD Publishing/ITF, Paris, http://dx.doi.org/10.1787/9789282107782-en.

OECD (forthcoming a), "Aligning Policies for the Transition to a Low-carbon Economy", OECD Publishing, Paris, http://dx.doi.org/10.1787/9789264233294-en.

OECD (forthcoming b), "Achieving a level playing field for International Investment in Green Energy", OECD Publishing, Paris.

OECD (forthcoming c), "Fostering Green Growth in Agriculture: The Role of Training, Advisory Services and Extension Initiatives", OECD Publishing, Paris, http://dx.doi.org/10.1787/9789264232198-en.

OECD (forthcoming d), "Biodiversity offsets: Effective Design and Implementation", OECD Publishing, Paris.

OECD (forthcoming e), "Climate Change Risks and Adaptation: Linking Policy and Economics", OECD, Paris.

OECD (2015a), *Policy Guidance for Investment in Clean Energy Infrastructure: Expanding Access to Clean Energy for Green Growth and Development,* OECD Publishing, Paris, http://dx.doi.org/10.1787/9789264212664-en.

OECD (2015b), *Mapping Channels to Mobilise Institutional Investment in Sustainable Energy,* Green Finance and Investment, OECD Publishing, Paris, http://dx.doi.org/10.1787/9789264224582-en.

OECD (2015c), "Domestic Incentive Measures for Environmental Goods with Possible Trade Implications: Electric Vehicles and Batteries", OECD Publishing, Paris, COM/TAD/ENV/JWPTE(2013)27/FINAL.

OECD (2015d), *Water Resources Allocation: Sharing Risks and Opportunities,* OECD Studies on Water, OECD Publishing, Paris, http://dx.doi.org/10.1787/9789264229631-en.

OECD (2015e), *Material Resources, Productivity and the Environment,* OECD Green Growth Studies, OECD Publishing, Paris, http://dx.doi.org/10.1787/9789264190504-en.

OECD (2015f), "Green Growth in Fisheries and Aquaculture", OECD Publishing, Paris, http://dx.doi.org/10.1787/9789264232143-en.

OECD (2014a), *Green Growth Indicators 2014,* OECD Green Growth Studies, OECD Publishing, Paris, http://dx.doi.org/10.1787/9789264202030-en.

OECD (2014b), *The Cost of Air Pollution: Health Impacts of Road Transport,* OECD Publishing, Paris, http://dx.doi.org/10.1787/9789264210448-en.
OECD (2014c), *Green Growth Indicators for Agriculture: A Preliminary Assessment,* OECD Green Growth Studies, OECD Publishing, Paris, http://dx.doi.org/10.1787/9789264223202-en.
OECD (2014d), "Municipal waste", *OECD Environment Statistics* (database), https://data.oecd.org/waste/municipal-waste.htm.
OECD (2014e), "Creating an Environment for Investment and Sustainable Development", in *Development Co-operation Report 2014: Mobilising Resources for Sustainable Development,* OECD Publishing, Paris, http://dx.doi.org/10.1787/dcr-2014-16-en.
OECD (2014f), "Finding Synergies for Environment and Development Finance", in *Development Co-operation Report 2014: Mobilising Resources for Sustainable Development,* OECD Publishing, Paris, http://dx.doi.org/10.1787/dcr-2014-22-en.
OECD (2014g), *Job Creation and Local Economic Development,* OECD Publishing, Paris, http://dx.doi.org/10.1787/9789264215009-en.
OECD (2013a), *Effective Carbon Prices,* OECD Publishing, Paris, http://dx.doi.org/10.1787/9789264196964-en.
OECD (2013b), *Taxing Energy Use: A Graphical Analysis,* OECD Publishing, Paris, http://dx.doi.org/10.1787/9789264183933-en.
OECD (2013c), *Inventory of Estimated Budgetary Support and Tax Expenditures for Fossil Fuels 2013,* OECD Publishing, Paris, http://dx.doi.org/10.1787/9789264187610-en.
OECD (2013d), *Long-term investors and green infrastructure: policy highlights,* OECD, Paris, www.oecd.org/env/cc/Investors%20in%20Green%20Infrastructure%20brochure%20(f)%20[lr].pdf.
OECD (2013e), *Policy Instruments to Support Green Growth in Agriculture,* OECD Green Growth Studies, OECD Publishing, http://dx.doi.org/10.1787/9789264203525-en.
OECD (2013f), *Scaling-up Finance Mechanisms for Biodiversity,* OECD Publishing, Paris, http://dx.doi.org/10.1787/9789264193833-en.
OECD (2013g), *Putting Green Growth at the Heart of Development,* OECD Green Growth Studies, OECD Publishing, http://dx.doi.org/10.1787/9789264181144-en.
OECD (2013h), *Green Growth in Cities,* OECD Green Growth Studies, OECD Publishing, Paris, http://dx.doi.org/10.1787/9789264195325-en.
OECD (2012a), *Mortality Risk Valuation in Environment, Health and Transport Policies,* OECD Publishing, Paris, http://dx.doi.org/10.1787/9789264130807-en.
OECD (2012b), *Energy,* OECD Green Growth Studies, OECD Publishing, Paris, http://www.oecd-ilibrary.org/environment/energy_9789264115118-en.
OECD (2012c), *Meeting the Water Reform Challenge,* OECD Studies on Water, OECD Publishing, Paris, http://dx.doi.org/10.1787/9789264170001-en.
OECD (2012d), *OECD Environmental Outlook to 2050: The Consequences of Inaction,* OECD Publishing, Paris, http://dx.doi.org/10.1787/9789264122246-en.
OECD (2012e), *Compact City Policies: A Comparative Assessment,* OECD Green Growth Studies, OECD Publishing, Paris, http://dx.doi.org/10.1787/9789264167865-en.
OECD (2012f), *Linking Renewable Energy to Rural Development,* OECD Green Growth Studies, OECD Publishing, Paris, http://dx.doi.org/10.1787/9789264180444-en.
OECD (2012g), OECD (2012), "The Jobs Potential of a Shift Towards a Low-Carbon Economy", *OECD Green Growth Papers,* No. 2012/01, OECD Publishing, Paris, http://dx.doi.org/10.1787/5k9h3630320v-en.
Poirier, J. et al. (2015), "The Benefits of International Co-authorship in Scientific Papers: The Case of Wind Energy Technologies", *OECD Environment Working Papers,* No. 81, OECD Publishing, Paris, http://dx.doi.org/10.1787/5js69ld9w9nv-en.
Roy, R. (2014), "Environmental and Related Social Costs of the Tax Treatment of Company Cars and Commuting Expenses", *OECD Environment Working Papers,* No. 70, OECD Publishing, Paris, http://dx.doi.org/10.1787/5jxwrr5163zp-en.
Sauvage, J. (2014), "The Stringency of Environmental Regulations and Trade in Environmental Goods", *OECD Trade and Environment Working Papers,* No. 2014/03, OECD Publishing, Paris, http://dx.doi.org/10.1787/5jxrjn7xsnmq-en.
TNO (2013), "Kansen voor een circulaire economie in Nederland" ["Opportunities for a circular economy in the Netherlands"], TNO, Delft, http://www.rijksoverheid.nl/bestanden/documenten-en-publicaties/rapporten/2013/06/20/tno-rapport-kansen-voor-de-circulaire-economie-in-nederland/tno-rapport-kansen-voor-de-circulaire-economie-in-nederland.pdf.
Wilson, L. et al. (2014), "The Role of National Ecosystem Assessments in Influencing Policy Making", *OECD Environment Working Papers,* No. 60, OECD Publishing, Paris, http://dx.doi.org/10.1787/5jxvl3zsbhkk-en.

1 "Competitiveness Impacts of the German Electricity Tax", COM/ENV/EPOC/CTPA/CFA(2014)19.
2 COM/ENV/EPOC/CTPA/CFA(2014)20.
3 ENV/EPOC/WPIEEP(2014)16.
4 www.oecd.org/greengrowth/ggsd-2014.htm.
5 http://gggi.org/.
6 http://www.unep.org/.
7 www.worldbank.org/.
8 www.greengrowthknowledge.org/.
9 www.oecd.org/greengrowth/Issue%20Note%20Session%20Two_final.pdf.
10 www.oecd.org/greengrowth/Issue%20Note%20Session%20One%20GGSD%20Forum.pdf.
11 www.oecd.org/futures/oceaneconomy.htm.

CHAPTER 4

THE VALUE OF **INSTITUTIONAL SETTINGS** FOR MAINSTREAMING GREEN GROWTH

This chapter describes how green growth is being implemented across the OECD work programme and examines how far the mainstreaming process has advanced since 2011, using OECD country surveillance series as a yardstick for progress across the Organisation (e.g. *OECD Economic Surveys, Environmental Performance Reviews, Investment Policy Reviews and Reviews of Innovation* Policy). The chapter draws a series of lessons from the rapid, but uneven mainstreaming process, to accelerate progress both at the OECD and for governments and other organisations working towards the mainstreaming of green growth.

Green growth mainstreaming has been rapid, but uneven across the OECD. Instructive lessons arise for both the Organisation and governments seeking to implement institutional mechanisms for green growth.

Great strides have been made in mainstreaming green growth within the OECD, but progress is uneven. What lessons can be learnt about the ongoing process? Green growth work at the OECD has rapidly accelerated, consistent with a concerted mainstreaming effort since the 2011 launch of the Green Growth Strategy. This chapter describes how green growth is being implemented across the OECD work programme. It examines how far mainstreaming has advanced in the past four years, using the OECD core country surveillance exercises that are relevant to green growth as a litmus test for progress. It considers lessons arising from wide variation in progress across publication series and issues: what mechanisms have spurred integration in some areas relative to others, and what lessons arise for governments, the OECD and other organisations? What are practical ways to tackle the full spectrum of green growth issues across all parts of the Organisation? The chapter also looks at ways to enhance the use of green growth indicators as a core mechanism for facilitating the mainstreaming process.

The rationale for considering ways to accelerate and streamline the mainstreaming process is twofold. The first rationale is to showcase lessons -from the OECD process for the benefit of governments and other institutions seeking to advance green growth. Governments could consider undertaking similar steps to those taken by the OECD, including meeting the challenge of co-ordinating across portfolios and ministries to align growth and environmental objectives. The OECD experience is instructive, particularly in those areas that have experienced rapid mainstreaming. The second rationale is to examine how lessons learnt can be applied in green growth work across the OECD, to maximise its impact across the board. The ultimate aim is to better support governments in implementing green growth.

Just as green growth strategies must be mainstreamed across government policies in order to succeed, the OECD considers that its advice must be coherent across policy domains to support governments. The Organisation has undertaken a conscious and deliberate process to drive and co-ordinate green growth across its work programme since the 2009 OECD Ministerial Declaration on Green Growth. Figure 4.1 provides an overview of the Organisation's governance arrangements, detailed below.

Highest-level strategic oversight involving a leadership role for economic and environmental policy makers. In line with the governance advice given to governments in the 2011 Green Growth Strategy, green growth work at the OECD is overseen at the highest levels of the Organisation, with strategic direction provided by the Deputy Secretary-General. Oversight is shared between the OECD Chief Economist, who helps drive integration of green growth objectives into the Organisation's broader economic policy advice, and the Environment Director.

Mechanisms to overcome institutional inertia and drive co-operation. Day-to-day oversight of the mainstreaming process is undertaken by a Green Growth Co-ordinator, who monitors and helps integrate green growth work across OECD committees, supported by a Green Growth Unit. The Unit is located in the Environment Directorate, but it takes its working directions from a Green Growth Core Group comprising senior representatives from the four main directorates leading green growth – the Economics Department, the Directorate for Science, Technology and Innovation, the Statistics Directorate and the Environment Directorate. Representatives from other directorates are added as needed. The Group meets two to three times a year to help guide the Organisation's green growth work and ensure its coherence. A senior economist in the Economics Department is dedicated full-time to co-ordinating and mainstreaming green growth into the Department's core economic policy advice to countries. Another senior economist works for both the Economics Department and the Environment Directorate, to bridge work undertaken across the two directorates on environmental policies and determinants of growth.

An informal grouping of interested OECD permanent representatives from delegations provides guidance on co-ordinating the Organisation's work from a country-delegate perspective. The "Friends of Green Growth" convene on an ad hoc basis, in person or by email, as required to support direction of the green growth work programme. They are an important link with countries to help develop a whole-of-government view on relevant issues.

Facilitating multidisciplinary dialogue and driving synergies on cross-cutting green growth issues: the Green Growth and Sustainable Development Forum. The Organisation's core substantive mechanism to drive green growth mainstreaming is the Green Growth and Sustainable Development (GGSD) Forum.[1] Held annually since 2012, the Forum addresses a different topic each year, convening experts from across policy areas on a subject-specific basis. Its first mission is to serve as a horizontal instrument to advance OECD green growth work, and in particular to identify gaps meriting further investigation by committees. The idea is to help identify knowledge gaps and design work programmes to address them. In addition to driving internal work, the GGSD Forum supports national policy making, by sharing policy analysis and experience across countries and sectors. The 2015 event, to be held on 14-15 December, will address the topic, "Enabling the next industrial revolution: Systems innovation for green growth". Previous events have focused on "Addressing the social implication of green growth" (2014), "How to unlock investment in support of green growth?" (2013) and "Encouraging the efficient and sustainable use of natural resources: Policy instruments and social acceptability" (2012).[2]

FIGURE 4.1 – GREEN GROWTH GOVERNANCE AT THE OECD

DEPUTY SECRETARY GENERAL
CHIEF ECONOMIST - ENVIRONMENT DIRECTOR

2 MECHANISMS TO DRIVE CO-OPERATION

GREEN GROWTH CO-ORDINATOR
GREEN GROWTH UNIT

GREEN GROWTH CORE GROUP

ECONOMICS DEPARTMENT
Dedicated bridging personnel

FRIENDS OF GREEN GROWTH
Informal group of permanent government representatives

GREEN GROWTH & SUSTAINABLE DEVELOPMENT FORUM

COMPRISES REPRESENTATIVES FROM:

- ECONOMICS DEPARTMENT
- DIRECTORATE FOR SCIENCE, TECHNOLOGY AND INNOVATION
- ENVIRONMENT DIRECTORATE
- STATISTICS DIRECTORATE
- CENTRE FOR TAX POLICY AND ADMINISTRATION
- DEVELOPMENT CO-OPERATION DIRECTORATE
- TRADE AND AGRICULTURE DIRECTORATE

HOW FAR HAS THE MAINSTREAMING PROCESS COME?

A litmus test for progress: OECD country surveillance. As the main country surveillance series relevant to green growth, the OECD *Economic Surveys, Investment Policy Reviews, Environmental Performance Reviews and Reviews of Innovation Policy* represent a proxy for how green growth mainstreaming is progressing across the OECD. *Economic Surveys* and *Environmental Performance Reviews*[3] are the results of mandatory review processes that apply to all OECD countries and have been progressively extended to key partners. *Reviews of Innovation Policy* are voluntary and *Investment Policy Reviews* relate only to partner and other economies. Taken as a whole, great strides have been made. Nearly 70% of the country reviews – or 80 of 115 reports – published since the launch of the Green Growth Strategy[4] feature policy recommendations that are relevant to green growth. These include concrete recommendations provided in executive summaries, assessment and recommendations sections, and chapter summaries. This work complements the considerable number of relevant sectoral and issue-specific publications (over 130 across policy areas) that have been released since 2011.

70% of country surveillance since 2011 features green growth recommendations.

The OECD country surveillance exercises suggest that mainstreaming is uneven across the Organisation. While progress is being made in some areas at a fast clip, more work is required in others. Since 2011, all *Environmental Performance Reviews* include a chapter dedicated to assessing progress towards green growth as one of their three core chapters (Figure 4.2); consequently, all 14 *Environmental Performance Reviews* analysed for this report contain green growth recommendations. Among the other publication series, 62 of the 76 *Economic Surveys* reviewed (around 82%) make recommendations relevant to green growth, compared to 4 of 13 *Investment Policy Reviews* (around 30%). None of the 12 *Reviews of Innovation Policy* do: this is despite significant work being undertaken on green innovation policy as part of other work streams in relevant committees (Chapter 3) and the importance of innovation policy for green growth, demonstrating scope for improvement.

Treatment of green growth issues differs significantly. Figure 4.3 illustrates how frequently various green growth issues are treated across country reviews. Unsurprisingly, the various policy instruments to price pollution and promote efficient resource use feature predominantly in OECD advice. The most commonly addressed issues are environmentally related tax reform (72 reviews), carbon-pricing mechanisms (60 reviews), green technology subsidies (53 reviews) and regulation providing incentives for green growth (51 reviews). Among the least-referenced issues is fossil-fuel subsidy reform (41 reviews). This is perhaps surprising, given the subsidies in both OECD countries and partner economies, and considering that the most frequently addressed issue – environmentally related tax reform – targets their elimination.

Energy (discussed in 73 of the 115 reports reviewed) is the clear front-runner when it comes to sectoral and issue-specific policy, followed by transport, innovation and climate change (discussed in around 50 reviews each). Despite representing a systemic risk to growth, biodiversity and ecosystem loss receives relatively little treatment (28 reviews). Investment and finance (43 reviews) could also reasonably be expected to play a larger role in the reviews, since an economy-wide transition will require substantial investment across green infrastructure sectors, such as renewable energy and other low-carbon means of generating electricity, energy efficiency, sustainable transport, water supply and sanitation, and buildings (Kaminker et al., 2013). Agriculture (32 reviews) and waste management (23 reviews) also receive relatively little attention.

Social implications of green growth are amongst the least-discussed issues in country surveillance.

One of the least-discussed issues is policy addressing the social implications of green growth: only 19 reviews discuss potential labour market impacts and 12 mention household impacts. As government policy is increasingly expected to address the equity implications of reform ex ante, and given the widely documented rise in income inequality in many OECD countries over the past three decades (OECD, 2011; Cingano, 2014), the distributional impacts of green growth could be expected to feature more prominently in OECD advice. Addressing the distributional implications of green growth on the poor is also essential to reform.

FIGURE 4.2 – GREEN GROWTH RECOMMENDATIONS IN COUNTRY SURVEILLANCE

Total number of reports 115 Reports with green growth recommendations 80

Environmental Performance Reviews 14
Reports with green growth recommendations 14

Economic Surveys 76
Reports with green growth recommendations 62

Investment Policy Reviews 13
Reports with green growth recommendations 4

Reviews of Innovation Policy 12
Reports with green growth recommendations 0

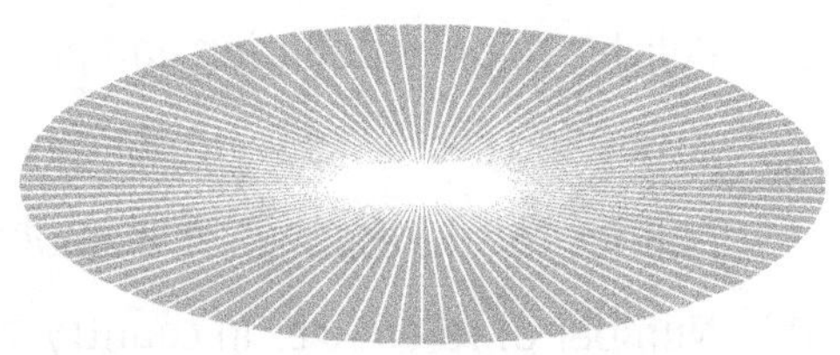

FIGURE 4.3 – REFERENCES TO GREEN GROWTH TOPICS IN COUNTRY SURVEILLANCE

Policies to price pollution and provide incentives for efficient resource use

Issue- and sector-specific policies

Policies to address the social implications of green growth

Number of references in country surveillance

The use of green growth indicators also varies widely, with some applied much more frequently than others. Figure 4.4 shows how the 2011 Green Growth Strategy indicators are being used across country surveillance exercises. The indicators are referenced over 415 times across the 115 reports reviewed, predominantly in *Environmental Performance Reviews* (237 references) and *Economic Surveys* (154). The share of renewables in energy supply – part of the energy productivity indicator – is the most common indicator, referenced in 48 of the 115 reviews. Environmentally related taxation (35 reviews) and carbon productivity (25 reviews)[5] are also common. Among the other frequently cited indicators are health impacts of environmental degradation and related costs (31 reviews), R&D expenditure relevant to green growth (22 reviews) and access to sewerage treatment and drinking water (22 reviews). This reflects work undertaken at the OECD to better quantify the health impacts of pollution and areas where data are readily available.

Nearly 80% of green growth indicators feature in less than 17% of country surveillance reports.

Overall, nearly 80% (or 23 of the 29) indicators and indicator sub-components are referenced in fewer than 20 country reviews – i.e. less than 17% of the documents reviewed. As is to be expected, green growth indicator use depends largely on their availability, comparability and capacity to be effectively understood and applied. Despite significant progress on several fronts in developing green growth indicators (Chapter 3), there are several indicators that are largely unmeasurable today. Understandably, these indicators receive relatively little treatment across country surveillance documents. As an example, some of the least-referenced indicators include production of environmental goods and services; water productivity; environmentally adjusted (multifactor) productivity (for an example of a report that considers this issue, see OECD, 2014a); the natural-resource index; and environment-related innovation. Each of these indicators is referenced in fewer than 5 of the 115 reports reviewed.

DRAWING LESSONS FROM PROGRESS TO DATE: GREEN GROWTH IN *ECONOMIC SURVEYS*

A number of mechanisms have driven the relatively rapid pace of green growth integration in *Economic Surveys*. The section below addresses the resulting lessons that are relevant both to governments and the OECD, and considers how they might be applied to advance mainstreaming green growth across the OECD, as potential examples for governments to draw on. While 100% of *Environmental Performance Reviews* have included green growth recommendations since 2011, the experience with the other surveys is more interesting from a mainstreaming perspective, as they are outside the core environmental work stream of the OECD.

Lesson No. 1: High-level strategic direction really does matter

The OECD Chief Economist is formally engaged in green growth mainstreaming, sharing oversight of the process with the Environment Director. Thus, the direction to integrate green growth objectives into the Economics Department's work comes from the top. The resulting lesson is that high-level strategic direction really does matter.

Applying the lesson to the OECD: there is potential to strengthen oversight of green growth across directorates. While green growth mainstreaming is overseen at the highest levels of the Organisation, heads of directorates are not currently directly implicated in green growth governance, with the exception of the Chief Economist and the Environment Director. The strategic direction of the Deputy Secretary-General, Chief Economist and Environment Director has played a critical role in driving integration of green growth across the Organisation as a whole. More direct implication of the heads of other core directorates, such as the Directorate for Science, Technology and Innovation and the Statistics Directorate, could promote more widespread diffusion of green growth across the Organisation.

FIGURE 4.4 – TREATMENT OF GREEN GROWTH INDICATORS IN COUNTRY SURVEILLANCE

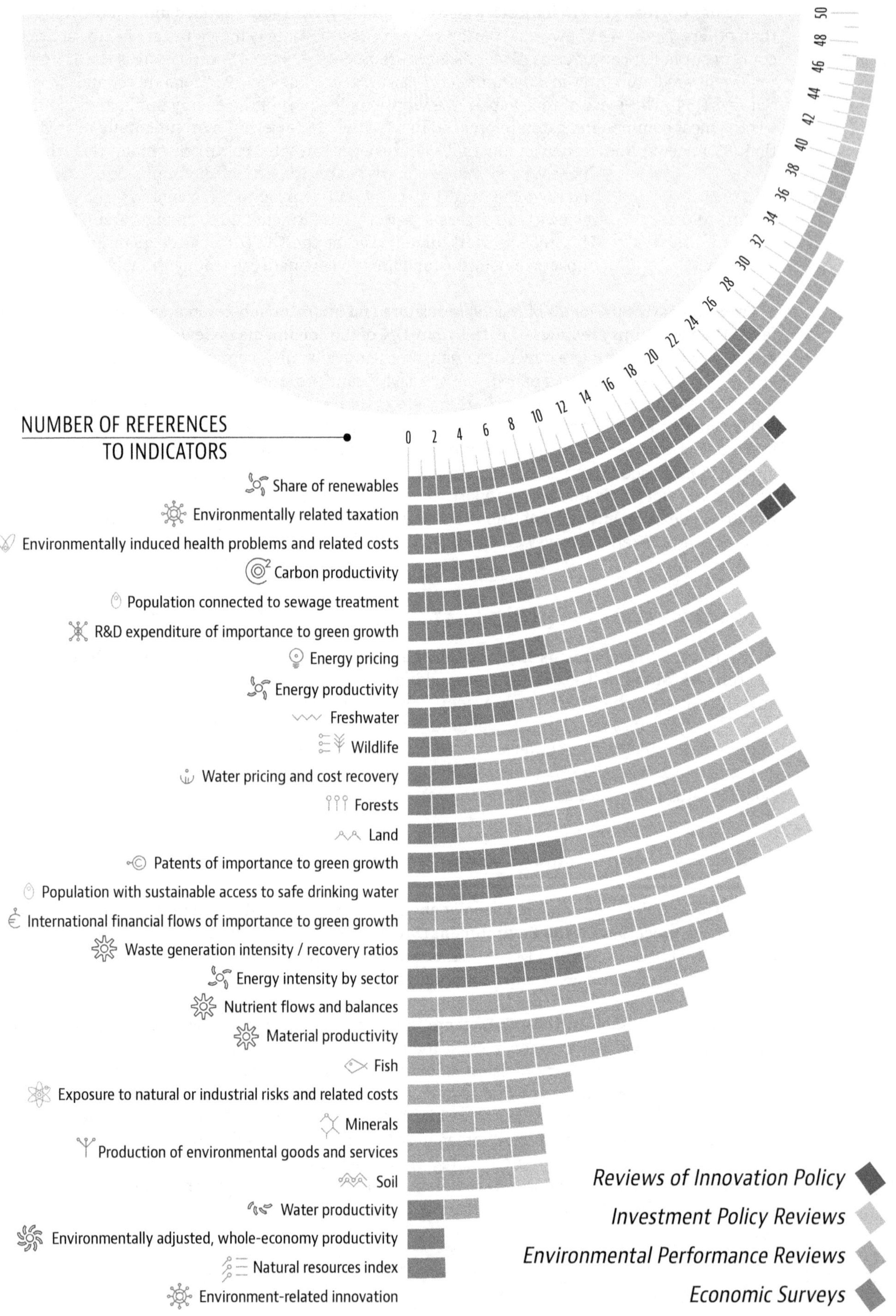

Lesson No. 2: Formalising institutional structures for mainstreaming and ensuring accountability in programmes of work and budget

Beyond the Environment Directorate, the Economics Department is the only OECD directorate to have formalised structures for mainstreaming. Green growth analysis is formally integrated into the Economics Department's two core substantive work areas, policy analysis and country studies. A dedicated work stream addresses green growth as part of structural policy analysis work in the Policy Studies Branch; a dedicated senior policy analyst oversees mainstreaming in country surveillance from the office of the head of the Country Studies Branch. The work undertaken in the Policy Studies Branch is delivered to its joint supervisors, the Economic Policy Committee and Environmental Policy Committee, which integrate it into their own programmes. The principal senior economist undertaking the work is shared by and responsible for bridging relevant analysis of the Economics Department and Environment Directorate. No formalised mechanisms for mainstreaming or co-operation exist for the Organisation's investment or innovation work. The lesson is that formal structures for co-ordination and collaboration – including shared staff – and clear accountability mechanisms can help drive mainstreaming. The Environment Directorate also shares a modeller with the International Energy Agency (IEA), with benefits accruing to both teams.

More formalised work programmes in relevant Directorates and dedicated resources can help drive mainstreaming.

Applying the lesson to the OECD: there is potential to strengthen oversight of green growth across directorates. Of the directorates responsible for the core surveillance series relevant to green growth, the Economics Department is the only one to have implemented formalised institutional structures for mainstreaming. Hence, there is scope to increase their use across the Organisation, through more formalised work streams focusing on green growth or human resources dedicated to the mainstreaming process.

Unless horizontal priorities are reflected in committee work programmes, directorates and their human resources have little incentive to action them, given their limited resources. As an Organisation-wide priority, green growth needs to be reflected in the work programmes of relevant committees. The vast majority of OECD committees are advancing green growth work and have a number of relevant projects reflected in their programmes of work and budgets, as demonstrated by the breadth of OECD green growth work addressed in Chapter 4. As Chapter 4 shows, the vast majority of OECD committees are advancing green growth work, and have undertaken a number of relevant projects. There are, however, some exceptions; a more firm requirement to reflect horizontal priorities in their work programmes is one potential way to help shift residual inertia in committees.

Greater committee collaboration could be envisaged. Currently, green growth work in the Economics Department is overseen to good effect by both the Economic Policy Committee and the Environmental Policy Committee. In other areas, more formalised joint committee structures supervise cross-committee work streams – for example, the Joint Meeting of Tax and Environment Experts brings together the Committee on Fiscal Affairs and the Environmental Policy Committee. Further joint meetings could be considered to drive work across multiple committees.

Changes to country surveillance processes could be considered to help support mainstreaming. *Economic Surveys* are undertaken for all OECD countries and key partner economies over an 18-24 month cycle. By contrast, *Environmental Performance Reviews* are undertaken approximately every decade. How these two core surveillance exercises can best relate to one another, given their different cycles, should be considered further. Experience with formalising climate change mitigation policy assessment in *Economic Surveys* as part of the lead-up to the United Nations Climate Change Conference (COP21) represents a testing ground for this proposal.[6] The development of short thematic reports drawing overarching cross-country lessons on green growth from *Economic Surveys, Environmental Performance Reviews, Investment Policy Reviews* and potentially also the *In-Depth Energy Policy Reviews* of the IEA could help highlight and guide future work on the major issues facing countries. They would also provide opportunities to feed lessons learnt from country experience back into the analysis being undertaken in relevant directorates.

Lesson No. 3: Providing a clear analytical framework for green growth

A clear analytical framework for mainstreaming exists in the Economics Department and its committees. Green growth has been integrated into the OECD *Going for Growth* publication series advising OECD and major emerging economy governments on priority structural economic reforms based on cross-country benchmarking. The series considers the implications of growth-enhancing policies for the environment and – since 2015 – the potential impacts of environmental degradation on the economy, affirming green growth as a fundamental growth issue. At the time of drafting, the Organisation's framework guidance on investment and innovation, the Policy Framework for Investment and the Innovation Strategy, are being updated to include guidance on green growth. The lesson is that a clear, overarching analytical framework for mainstreaming can play an important role in direction-setting. Inclusion of green growth in the Organisation's investment and innovation framework documents would help improve reflection of green growth issues in the relevant country surveillance series.

An Organisation-level analytical framework for green growth could help drive change.

Applying the lesson to the OECD: a single narrative should be developed and a clear analytical framework for green growth established at the Organisation level. No analytical framework articulating the role of green growth within the context of the Organisation-wide work programme currently exists, even though the number of cross-cutting initiatives is increasing. In addition to the Green Growth horizontal work programme, the Organisation's Inclusive Growth and New Approaches to Economic Challenges initiatives, as well as the well-being framework developed in the context of the OECD Better Life Initiative, are relevant. The initiatives aim to revisit traditional economic models by incorporating non-income dimensions of well-being – including environmental conditions – into policy design and considering their distributional implications.

The proliferation of cross-cutting analytical frameworks adds impetus to the need to clearly articulate how the Organisation's green growth work and other initiatives relate to one another within the broader work programme. The OECD@100 project – which combines modelling tools to provide a multidimensional, structured framework for thinking about the future - could be considered as a possible mechanism to articulate the interaction of various OECD-wide work priorities, including green growth. The project's *Policy Challenges for the Next 50 Years* publication provides insights into future trends and tensions likely to shape the policy environment over the next 50 years. The mega-trends identified include environmental pressures such as climate change and resource depletion, technological progress, long-term demographic shifts, growing urbanisation and rising inequalities. OECD modelling work has not yet developed a green growth scenario comprising a fuller suite of policy measures required to expand the green growth transition beyond renewables, as well as address climate change and the transition's overall impacts on the economy. Dedicated modelling work could be required to support full integration of green growth into such an initiative.

Lesson No. 4: Boosting resources dedicated to mainstreaming

The Economics Department is the only OECD directorate to have dedicated full-time senior personnel to the mainstreaming process and bridging personnel with the Environment Directorate; the impact shows. The lesson is that mainstreaming horizontal initiatives takes time and requires human resources dedicated to co-ordinating and overseeing integration of green growth principles into work programmes. Resources are also needed to help raise awareness of relevant work and enhance the interface with other directorates to ensure work undertaken elsewhere in the Organisation is clearly communicated to analysts.

Applying the lesson to the OECD: a concerted effort to formalise institutional structures for mainstreaming within directorates, in accordance with Lesson 2, would help ensure that sufficient resources are allocated to mainstreaming. The number of country reports since 2011 – over 115 – illustrates the need for dedicated resourcing in core directorates if mainstreaming is to be effective. The total amount of resources needed is not the central issue, as it will often be small. Rather, the very allocation of resources ensures follow-up.

FACILITATING TREATMENT OF A FULL SPECTRUM OF GREEN GROWTH ISSUES

Ensuring a comprehensive approach to green growth. The variation in the treatment of green growth issues in country analyses suggests that practical mechanisms are required to optimise substantive links and encourage sharing relevant information across policy areas.

Lesson No. 5: Ensuring mechanisms to encourage information sharing and optimise policy linkages to facilitate treatment of a full spectrum of green growth issues

Applying the lesson to the OECD: template guidance, checklists or charts of green growth issues for routine consideration in country surveillance documents can help ensure principal recommendations made in one directorate are picked up in relevant analysis in others. These could be vetted and routinely updated by relevant committees. Direct input of relevant directorates into the questionnaires sent to countries in preparation for country surveillance reports is another potential mechanism.

Practical mechanisms are needed to optimise policy linkages and encourage information sharing.

Greater use of inter-directorate collaboration in drafting and finalising documents is also relevant. For example, where *Environmental Performance Reviews* address innovation issues, the analysis should arguably be supported by colleagues undertaking relevant work in the Directorate for Science, Technology and Innovation; broader coverage of green growth information – both across the Organisation and across issues – would likely result. Greater use of dedicated or bridging personnel would help connect work across committees and directorates.

Resolving issues of terminology is a basic but fundamental mechanism to help clarify linkages and synergies between different work programmes. Currently, the OECD works on green infrastructure; clean energy infrastructure; and low-carbon, climate-resilient infrastructure, for example. Resolving where related work areas intersect and clarifying basic terminology can facilitate information sharing among work streams, directorates and committees.

A green growth policy database would facilitate information sharing. This database could draw inspiration from the IEA Policies and Measures databases bringing together country policies on climate change, renewable energy and energy efficiency.[7] The Green Growth Knowledge Platform is one potential international partner that would be well placed to develop such a database with the OECD.

ENHANCING USE OF GREEN GROWTH INDICATORS

The relatively limited number of OECD green growth indicators used in country surveys warrants attention because of their importance in facilitating mainstreaming. Mainstreaming green growth indicators is challenging on a number of fronts. The most fundamental challenge is that the methodological development of the OECD green growth indicator framework is ongoing, including with respect to the six headline indicators proposed in *Green Growth Indicators 2014* (OECD, 2014b). Despite considerable advances in the measurement agenda since 2011, 4 of the headline indicators and around 20% of the more comprehensive set of 26 indicators are not yet methodologically ripe for use. Thus in many cases, proposed indicators cannot yet be reflected in country and policy analysis. A second challenge is that even if methodological development of indicators is complete, data gaps may mean that they cannot be produced for all countries, limiting their use in analysis. Country efforts to adapt the OECD green growth indicator framework to help track national progress towards green growth objectives are ongoing, as are data gathering efforts; about 50% of the more comprehensive set of 26 indicators cannot be currently produced for most OECD countries due to data gaps. This means that countries are likely to experience the same issues as the OECD in integrating green growth indicators into policy analysis.

Lesson No. 6: Promoting a subset of measureable green growth indicators to enhance indicator use

The basic issue is how to promote use of green growth-relevant indicators in analysis, even as the measurement agenda and data gathering efforts advance. Where good-quality data is not yet available, preliminary estimates can be used for some countries with appropriate caveats, assuming the conceptual development of indicators is complete. A subset of currently measureable green growth indicators should be encouraged, to maintain momentum on green growth implementation by countries.

Applying the lesson to the OECD: the subset of agreed and measurable green growth indicators could form part of template guidance provided to relevant directorates, to be vetted potentially by the Environmental Policy Committee and other relevant committees. The indicators could include green growth-relevant indicators developed in other parts of the Organisation, such as the Environmental Policy Stringency and Burdens on the Economy due to Environmental Policies indicators developed by the Economics Department's green growth team and the Environment Directorate (Chapter 3). Furthermore, the vetted subset of measurable green growth indicators could be disseminated and used in country and policy analysis to further enhance the use of green growth indicators across the Organisation.

MAXIMISING IMPACT: NEXT STEPS FOR MAINSTREAMING

The mainstreaming measures that have worked well in the Economics Department and its Committees provide a good platform to assess and fine-tune integration efforts in other parts of the OECD. A first step would be to undertake a review of institutional settings in core directorates against the mechanisms used by the Economics Department and its committees to mainstream green growth. Taking stock of green growth-related elements of committee work and work relevant for "export" to other committees could help start the process of strengthening substantive links and information sharing across the Organisation. The Green Growth Unit could assist in this process.

The lessons learnt from successful mainstreaming measures in the Economics Department provide useful pointers to governments seeking to implement institutional structures to advance green growth. The most important elements include establishing high-level leadership and clear accountabilities; creating formal structures for co-ordination and collaboration; clearly articulating how green growth links to other policy priorities; and dedicating human resources to mainstreaming in organisations important to green growth. Governments need to ensure that information is shared across policy areas and ministries, and that robust indicators are used to chart progress.

CHAPTER REFERENCES

Cingano, F. (2014), "Trends in Income Inequality and its Impact on Economic Growth", *OECD Social, Employment and Migration Working Papers,* No. 163, OECD Publishing, Paris, http://dx.doi.org/10.1787/5jxrjncwxv6j-en.

Kaminker, C. et al. (2013), "Institutional Investors and Green Infrastructure Investments: Selected Case Studies", *OECD Working Papers on Finance, Insurance and Private Pensions,* No. 35, OECD Publishing, Paris, http://dx.doi.org/10.1787/5k3xr8k6jb0n-en.

OECD (2014a), *OECD Economic Surveys: Norway 2014*, OECD Publishing, Paris, http://dx.doi.org/10.1787/eco_surveys-nor-2014-en.

OECD (2014b), *Green Growth Indicators 2014*, OECD Green Growth Studies, OECD Publishing, Paris, http://dx.doi.org/10.1787/9789264202030-en.

OECD (2011), *Divided We Stand: Why Inequality Keeps Rising,* OECD Publishing, Paris, http://dx.doi.org/10.1787/9789264119536-en.

1 See www.oecd.org/greengrowth/ggsd-forum.htm.

2 Further details on past events are available at www.oecd.org/greengrowth/ggsd-forum.htm. The 2016 event will focus on "Spatial Planning, Land-use and Urban Green Growth".

3 Economic Surveys and Environmental Performance Reviews are mandatory for all OECD countries and have been extended to key partners. Reviews of Innovation Policy are voluntary. Investment Policy Reviews apply mostly to OECD partner economies.

4 Reviews published between the launch of the Green Growth Strategy and 4 February 2015. The Economic Surveys and Environmental Performance Reviews are routinely undertaken for OECD countries and selected partner economies; the Reviews of Innovation Policy and Investment Policy Reviews are undertaken on an ad hoc basis and their content is largely demand-driven.

5 GDP generated per unit of carbon dioxide (CO2) emitted in production and real income per unit of CO2 emitted.

6 Treatment of climate change mitigation policy in Economic Surveys has been formalised since March 2014 as part of OECD preparations in the lead-up to the 2015 international climate change negotiations (COP21, scheduled for November 2015, Paris). All Economic Surveys are now complemented by a "technical background paper" on climate change mitigation that will feed into an online tool for COP21.

7 www.iea.org/policiesandmeasures/.

BIBLIOGRAPHY

COUNTRY REVIEWED	ECONOMIC SURVEYS	ENVIRONMENTAL PERFORMANCE REVIEWS	INVESTMENT POLICY REVIEWS	REVIEWS OF INNOVATION POLICY	IEA IN-DEPTH ENERGY POLICY REVIEWS*
Australia	2012, '14				2012
Austria	2011, '13	2013			2014
Belgium	2011, '13 '15				
Brazil	2011, '13				
Botswana			2014		
Canada	2012, '14				
Chile	2012, '13				2009
China People's Rep.	2013				
Colombia	2013, '15	2014	2012	2014	
Costa Rica			2013		
Croatia				2013	
Czech Republic	2011, '14				2010
Denmark	2012, '13				2011
Estonia	2012, '15				2013
Euro Area	2012, '14				
European Union	2012, '14				2014
Finland	2012, '14				2013
France	2013			2014	
Germany	2012, '14	2012			2013
Greece	2011, '13				2011
Hungary	2012, '14				2011
Iceland	2011, '13	2014			
India	2011, '14				
Indonesia	2012				
Ireland	2011, '13				2012
Israel	2011, '13	2011			
Italy	2013	2013			
Japan	2013				
Jordan			2013		
Kazakhstan			2012		
Korea	2012, '14			2014	2012
Luxembourg	2012				2014
Malaysia			2013		
Mauritius			2014		
Mexico	2013, '15	2013		2013	
Morocco					2014
Mozambique			2013		
Myanmar			2014		
Netherlands	2012, '14			2014	2014
New Zealand	2013				
Norway	2012, '14	2011			2011
Peru				2011	
Poland	2012, '14	2015			2011
Portugal	2012, '14	2011			
Russian Federation	2011, '14			2011	2014
Slovak Republic	2012, '14	2011			2012
Slovenia	2013	2012		2012	
South Africa	2013	2013			
Soutaheast Asia				2013	
Spain	2012, '14				
Sweden	2012	2014		2012	2013
Switzerland	2012, '13				2012
Tanzania			2013		
Tunisia			2012		
Turkey	2012, '14				
Ukraine			2011		2012
United Kingdom	2013				2012
United States	2012, '14				2014
Vietnam				2014	
Zambia			2012		

* Although not reviewed as part of this report, these references outline the *In-Depth Energy Policy Review* (IDR) series of the IEA as broader country analysis within the OECD organisational structure relevant to green growth. Traditionally, the IDRs include policy recommendations on energy efficiency, renewable energy and energy research and development towards green growth (see www.iea.org/countries/membercountries/). The primary focus of the report is on the OECD country surveillance documents. Integrating green growth into the OECD *Economic Surveys, Reviews of Innovation Policy, Investment Policy Reviews* and *Environmental Policy Reviews* was a forward work priority established in the 2011 Green Growth Strategy

2011 OECD Green Growth Strategy Package

- OECD (2011a), *Tools for Delivering on Green Growth,* prepared for the OECD Meeting of the Council at Ministerial Level, 25-26 May, 2011, http://www.oecd.org/greengrowth/48012326.pdf.
- OECD (2011b), *Towards Green Growth,* OECD Green Growth Studies, OECD Publishing, Paris, http://dx.doi.org/10.1787/9789264111318-en.
- OECD (2011c), *Towards Green Growth: A Summary for Policy Makers,* brochure prepared the OECD Meeting of the Council at Ministerial Level, 25-26 May, 2011, http://www.oecd.org/greengrowth/48012345.pdf.
- OECD (2011d), *Towards Green Growth: Monitoring Progress: OECD Indicators,* OECD Green Growth Studies, OECD Publishing, Paris, http://dx.doi.org/10.1787/9789264111356-en.

Green Growth Studies

- OECD (2015a), "Green Growth in Fisheries and Aquaculture", OECD Green Growth Studies, OECD Publishing, Paris. http://dx.doi.org/10.1787/9789264232143-en.
- OECD/Cedefop (2014), *Greener Skills and Jobs*, OECD Green Growth Studies, OECD Publishing, Paris, http://dx.doi.org/10.1787/9789264208704-en.
- OECD (2014a), *Green Growth Indicators for Agriculture:* A *Preliminary* Assessment, OECD Green Growth Studies, OECD Publishing, Paris, http://dx.doi.org/10.1787/9789264223202-en.
- OECD (2014b), *Green Growth Indicators 2014*, OECD Green Growth Studies, OECD Publishing, Paris, http://dx.doi.org/10.1787/9789264202030-en.
- OECD (2014c), *Towards Green Growth in Southeast Asia*, OECD Green Growth Studies, OECD Publishing, Paris, http://dx.doi.org/10.1787/9789264224100-en.
- OECD (2013a), *Green Growth in Cities*, OECD Green Growth Studies, OECD Publishing, Paris, http://dx.doi.org/10.1787/9789264195325-en.
- OECD (2013b), *Green Growth in Kitakyushu, Japan*, OECD Green Growth Studies, OECD Publishing, Paris, http://dx.doi.org/10.1787/9789264195134-en.
- OECD (2013c), *Green Growth in Stockholm, Sweden*, OECD Green Growth Studies, OECD Publishing, Paris, http://dx.doi.org/10.1787/9789264195158-en.
- OECD (2013d), *Policy Instruments to Support Green Growth in Agriculture*, OECD Green Growth Studies, OECD Publishing, Paris, http://dx.doi.org/10.1787/9789264203525-en.
- OECD (2013e), *Putting Green Growth at the Heart of Development*, OECD Green Growth Studies, OECD Publishing, Paris, http://dx.doi.org/10.1787/9789264181144-en.
- OECD (2012a), *Compact City Policies:* A Comparative Assessment, OECD Green Growth Studies, OECD Publishing, Paris, http://dx.doi.org/10.1787/9789264167865-en.
- OECD (2012b), *Energy*, OECD Green Growth Studies, OECD Publishing, Paris, http://www.oecd-ilibrary.org/environment/energy_9789264115118-en.
- OECD (2012c), *Linking Renewable Energy to Rural Development*, OECD Green Growth Studies, OECD Publishing, Paris, http://dx.doi.org/10.1787/9789264180444-en.

- OECD (2011a), *Food and Agriculture*, OECD Green Growth Studies, OECD Publishing, Paris, http://dx.doi.org/10.1787/9789264107250-en.
- OECD (2011b), *Fostering Innovation for Green Growth*, OECD Green Growth Studies, OECD Publishing, Paris, http://dx.doi.org/10.1787/9789264119925-en.

Green Growth Papers

- Bass, S., et al. (2013), "Making Growth Green and Inclusive: The Case of Ethiopia", *OECD Green Growth Papers*, No. 2013/07, OECD Publishing, Paris, http://dx.doi.org/10.1787/5k46dbzhrkhl-en.
- Beltramello, A. (2012), "Market Development for Green Cars", *OECD Green Growth Papers*, No. 2012/03, OECD Publishing, Paris, http://dx.doi.org/10.1787/5k95xtcmxltc-en.
- Beltramello, A., L. Haie-Fayle and D. Pilat (2013),"Why New Business Models Matter for Green Growth", *OECD Green Growth Papers*, No. 2013/01, OECD Publishing, Paris, http://dx.doi.org/10.1787/5k97gk40v3ln-en.
- Braathen, N.A. (2011), "Interactions Between Emission Trading Systems and Other Overlapping Policy Instruments", *OECD Green Growth Papers*, No. 2011/02, OECD Publishing, Paris, http://dx.doi.org/10.1787/5k97gk44c6vf-en.
- Banister, D., P. Crist and S. Perkins (2015), "Land Transport and How to Unlock Investment in Support of "Green Growth"", *OECD Green Growth Papers*, No. 2015/01, OECD Publishing, Paris, http://dx.doi.org/10.1787/5js65xnk52kc-en.
- Casado-Asensio, J. et al. (2014), "Green Development Co-operation in Zambia: An Overview", *OECD Green Growth Papers*, No. 2014/03, OECD Publishing, Paris, http://dx.doi.org/10.1787/5js6b25c2r5g-en.
- Glachant, M. (2013), "Greening Global Value Chains: Innovation and the International Diffusion of Technologies and Knowledge", *OECD Green Growth Papers*, No. 2013/05, OECD Publishing, Paris, http://dx.doi.org/10.1787/5k483jn87hnv-en.
- Kamp-Roelands, N. (2013), "Private Sector Initiatives on Measuring and Reporting on Green Growth", *OECD Green Growth Papers*, No. 2013/06, OECD Publishing, Paris, http://dx.doi.org/10.1787/5k483jn5j1lv-en.
- Martinez-Fernandez, C. et al. (2013), "Improving the Effectiveness of Green Local Development: The Role and Impact of Public Sector-Led Initiatives in Renewable Energy", *OECD Green Growth Papers*, No. 2013/09, OECD Publishing, Paris, http://dx.doi.org/10.1787/5k3w6ljtrj0q-en.
- Mohammed, E.Y., S. Wang and G. Kawaguchi (2013), "Making Growth Green and Inclusive: The Case of Cambodia", *OECD Green Growth Papers*, No. 2013/08, OECD Publishing, Paris, http://dx.doi.org/10.1787/5k420651szzr-en.
- OECD (2013a), "Building Green Global Value Chains: Committed Public-Private Coalitions in Agro-Commodity Markets", *OECD Green Growth Papers*, No. 2013/03, OECD Publishing, Paris, http://dx.doi.org/10.1787/5k483jndzwtj-en.
- OECD (2013b), "What Have We Learned from Attempts to Introduce Green-Growth Policies?", *OECD Green Growth Papers*, No. 2013/02, OECD Publishing, Paris, http://dx.doi.org/10.1787/5k486rchlnxx-en.
- OECD (2012a), "Green Growth and Environmental Governance in Eastern Europe, Caucasus, and Central Asia", *OECD Green Growth Papers*, No. 2012/02, OECD Publishing, Paris, http://dx.doi.org/10.1787/5k97gk42q86g-en.
- OECD (2012b), "The Jobs Potential of a Shift Towards a Low-Carbon Economy", *OECD Green Growth Papers*, No. 2012/01, OECD Publishing, Paris, http://dx.doi.org/10.1787/5k9h3630320v-en.
- Sinclair-Desgagné, B. (2013), "Greening Global Value Chains: Implementation Challenges", *OECD Green Growth Papers*, No. 2013/04, OECD Publishing, Paris, http://dx.doi.org/10.1787/5k483jnbjbzn-en.

Selected OECD Working Papers relevant to green growth

- Agrawala, Agrawala, S. et al. (2011), "Private Sector Engagement in Adaptation to Climate Change: Approaches to Managing Climate Risks", *OECD Environment Working Papers*, No. 39, OECD Publishing, Paris, http://dx.doi.org/10.1787/5kg221jkf1g7-en.

- Albrizio, S., T. Koźluk and V. Zipperer (2014), "Empirical Evidence on the Effects of Environmental Policy Stringency on Productivity Growth", *OECD Economics Department Working Papers*, No. 1179, OECD Publishing, Paris, http://dx.doi.org/10.1787/5jxrjnb36b40-en.

- Arlinghaus, J. (2015), "Impacts of Carbon Pricing on Indicators of Competitiveness: A Review of Empirical Findings", *OECD Environment Working Papers*, No. 87, OECD Publishing, Paris, http://dx.doi.org/10.1787/5js37p21grzq-en.

- Ang, G. and V. Marchal (2013), "Mobilising Private Investment in Sustainable Transport: The Case of Land-Based Passenger Transport Infrastructure", *OECD Environment Working Papers*, No. 56, OECD Publishing, Paris, http://doi.org/10.1787/5k46hjm8jpmv-en.

- Bahar, H., J. Egeland and R. Steenblik (2013), "Domestic Incentive Measures for Renewable Energy With Possible Trade Implications", *OECD Trade and Environment Working Papers*, No. 2013/01, OECD Publishing, Paris, http://dx.doi.org/10.1787/5k44srlksr6f-en.

- Bahar, H. and J. Sauvage (2013), "Cross-Border Trade in Electricity and the Development of Renewables Based Electric Power: Lessons from Europe", *OECD Trade and Environment Working Papers*, No. 2013/02, OECD Publishing, Paris, http://doi.org/10.1787/5k4869cdwnzr-en.

- Béné, C. et al. (2014), "Social Protection and Climate Change", OECD Development Co-operation Working Papers, No. 16, OECD Publishing, Paris, http://dx.doi.org/10.1787/5jz2qc8wc1s5-en.

- Botta, E. and T. Koźluk (2014), "Measuring Environmental Policy Stringency in OECD Countries: A Composite Index Approach", *OECD Economics Department Working Papers*, No. 1177, OECD Publishing, Paris, http://dx.doi.org/10.1787/5jxrjnc45gvg-en.

- Cárdenas Rodríguez, M., et al. (2014), "Inducing Private Finance for Renewable Energy Projects: Evidence from Micro-Data", *OECD Environment Working Papers*, No. 67, OECD Publishing, Paris, http://dx.doi.org/10.1787/5jxvg0k6thr1-en.

- Chateau, J., B. Magné and L. Cozzi (2014), "Economic Implications of the IEA Efficient World Scenario", *OECD Environment Working Papers*, No. 64, OECD Publishing, Paris, http://dx.doi.org/10.1787/5jz2qcn29lbw-en.

- Convery, F.J., L. Dunne and D. Joyce (2013), "Ireland's Carbon Tax and the Fiscal Crisis: Issues in Fiscal Adjustment, Environmental Effectiveness, Competitiveness, Leakage and Equity Implications", *OECD Environment Working Papers*, No. 59, OECD Publishing, Paris, http://dx.doi.org/10.1787/5k3z11j3w0bw-en.

- Corfee-Morlot, J. et al. (2012),"Towards a Green Investment Policy Framework: The Case of Low-Carbon, Climate-Resilient Infrastructure", *OECD Environment Working Papers*, No. 48, OECD Publishing, Paris, http://dx.doi.org/10.1787/5k8zth7s6s6d-en.

- de Serres, A. and F. Murtin (2011), "A Welfare Analysis of Climate Change Mitigation Policies", *OECD Economics Department Working Papers*, No. 908, OECD Publishing, Paris, http://dx.doi.org/10.1787/5kg0t00hd0g3-en.

- Dechezleprêtre, A., I. Haščič and N. Johnstone (2015), "Invention and International Diffusion of Water Conservation and Availability Technologies: Evidence from Patent Data", *OECD Environment Working Papers*, No. 82, OECD Publishing, Paris, http://dx.doi.org/10.1787/5js679fvllhg-en.

- Della Croce, R., C. Kaminker and F. Stewart (2011), "The Role of Pension Funds in Financing Green Growth Initiatives", *OECD Working Papers on Finance, Insurance and Private Pensions*, No. 0, OECD Publishing, Paris, http://dx.doi.org/10.1787/5kg58j1lwdjd-en.

- Dellink, R. et al. (2014), "Consequences of Climate Change Damages for Economic Growth: A Dynamic Quantitative Assessment", *OECD Economics Department Working Papers*, No. 1135, OECD Publishing, Paris, http://dx.doi.org/10.1787/5jz2bxb8kmf3-en.

- Drutschinin, A. and K. Casado-Asensio (forthcoming), "Biodiversity and Development Co-operation", *OECD Development Co-operation Working Papers*, OECD Publishing, Paris.

- Egli, F., C. Menon and N. Johnstone (forthcoming), "Quality and Breakthrough Inventions: The Case of Climate Mitigation Technologies", *OECD Science, Technology and Industry Working Papers*, OECD Publishing, Paris.

- George, C. (2013), "Developments in Regional Trade Agreements and the Environment: 2012 Update", *OECD Trade and Environment Working Papers*, No. 2013/04, OECD Publishing, Paris, http://dx.doi.org/10.1787/5k43m4nxwm25-en.

- Greene, J. and N.A. Braathen (2014), "Tax Preferences for Environmental Goals: Use, Limitations and Preferred Practices", *OECD Environment Working Papers*, No. 71, OECD Publishing, Paris, http://dx.doi.org/10.1787/5jxwrr4hkd6l-en.

- Harding, M. (2014), "The Diesel Differential: Differences in the Tax Treatment of Gasoline and Diesel for Road Use", *OECD Taxation Working Papers*, No. 21, OECD Publishing, Paris, http://dx.doi.org/10.1787/5jz14cd7hk6b-en.

- Harrison, K. (2013), "The Political Economy of British Columbia's Carbon Tax", *OECD Environment Working Papers*, No. 63, OECD Publishing, Paris, http://dx.doi.org/10.1787/5k3z04gkkhkg-en.

- Haščič, I., N. Johnstone and N. Kahrobaie (2012), "International Technology Agreements for Climate Change: Analysis Based on Co-Invention Data", *OECD Environment Working Papers*, No. 42, OECD Publishing, Paris, http://dx.doi.org/10.1787/5k9fgpw5tt9s-en.

- Haščič, I., J. Silva and N. Johnstone (2012), "Climate Mitigation and Adaptation in Africa: Evidence from Patent Data", *OECD Environment Working Papers*, No. 50, OECD Publishing, Paris, http://dx.doi.org/10.1787/5k8zng5smxjg-en.

- Haščič, I. et al. (2015), "Public Interventions and Private Climate Finance Flows: Empirical Evidence from Renewable Energy Financing", *OECD Environment Working Papers*, No. 80, OECD Publishing, Paris, http://dx.doi.org/10.1787/5js6b1r9lfd4-en.

- Inderst, G., C. Kaminker and F. Stewart (2012), "Defining and Measuring Green Investments: Implications for Institutional Investors' Asset Allocations", *OECD Working Papers on Finance, Insurance and Private Pensions*, No. 24, OECD Publishing, Paris, http://dx.doi.org/10.1787/5k9312twnn44-en.

- Kaminker, C. et al. (2013), "Institutional Investors and Green Infrastructure Investments: Selected Case Studies", *OECD Working Papers on Finance, Insurance and Private Pensions*, No. 35, OECD Publishing, Paris, http://dx.doi.org/10.1787/5k3xr8k6jb0n-en.

- Kaminker, C. and F. Stewart (2012), "The Role of Institutional Investors in Financing Clean Energy", *OECD Working Papers on Finance, Insurance and Private Pensions*, No. 23, OECD Publishing, Paris, http://dx.doi.org/10.1787/5k9312v21l6f-en.

- Kauffmann C., C. Tébar Less and D. Teichmann (2012), "Corporate Greenhouse Gas Emission Reporting: A Stocktaking of Government Schemes", *OECD Working Papers on International Investment*, No. 2012/01, OECD Publishing, Paris, http://dx.doi.org/10.1787/5k97g3x674lq-en.

- King, M. (2013), "Green Growth and Poverty Reduction: Policy Coherence for Pro-poor Growth", *OECD Development Co-operation Working Papers*, No. 14, OECD Publishing, Paris, http://dx.doi.org/10.1787/5k3ttg45wb31-en.

- Koźluk, T. and V. Zipperer (2013), "Environmental Policies and Productivity Growth: A Critical Review of Empirical Findings", *OECD Economics Department Working Papers*, No. 096, OECD Publishing, Paris, http://dx.doi.org/10.1787/5k3w725lhgf6-en.

- Koźluk, T. (2014), "The Indicators of the Economic Burdens of Environmental Policy Design: Results from the OECD Questionnaire", *OECD Economics Department Working Papers*, No. 1178, OECD Publishing, Paris, http://dx.doi.org/10.1787/5jxrjnbnbm8v-en.

- Lanzi, E. et al. (2013),"Addressing Competitiveness and Carbon Leakage Impacts Arising from Multiple Carbon Markets: A Modelling Assessment", *OECD Environment Working Papers*, No. 58, OECD Publishing, Paris, http://dx.doi.org/10.1787/5k40ggjj7z8v-en.

- Martinez-Fernandez, C., et al. (2013), "Green Growth in the Benelux: Indicators of Local Transition to a Low-Carbon Economy in Cross-Border Regions", *OECD Local Economic and Employment Development (LEED) Working Papers*, No. 2013/09, OECD Publishing, Paris, http://dx.doi.org/10.1787/5k453xgh72ls-en.

- Martinez-Fernandez, C. et al. (2013), "Measuring the Potential of Local Green Growth: An Analysis of Greater Copenhagen", *OECD Local Economic and Employment Development (LEED) Working Papers*, No. 2013/01, OECD Publishing, Paris, http://dx.doi.org/10.1787/5k4dhp0xzg26-en.

- Mazur, E. (2012), "Green Transformation of Small Businesses: Achieving and Going Beyond Environmental Requirements", *OECD Environment Working Papers*, No. 47, OECD Publishing, Paris, http://dx.doi.org/10.1787/5k92r8nmfgxp-en.

- Mullan, M. et al. (2013), "National Adaptation Planning: Lessons from OECD Countries", *OECD Environment Working Papers*, No. 54, OECD Publishing, Paris, http://dx.doi.org/10.1787/5k483jpfpsq1-en.

- OECD (2013c), "Biotechnology for the Environment in the Future: Science, Technology and Policy", *OECD Science, Technology and Industry Policy Papers*, No. 3, OECD Publishing, Paris, http://dx.doi.org/10.1787/5k4840hqhp7j-en.

- OECD (2013d), "Nanotechnology for Green Innovation", *OECD Science, Technology and Industry Policy Papers*, No. 5, OECD Publishing, Paris, http://dx.doi.org/10.1787/5k450q9j8p8q-en.

- Poirier, J. et al. (2015), "The Benefits of International Co-authorship in Scientific Papers: The Case of Wind Energy Technologies", *OECD Environment Working Papers*, No. 81, OECD Publishing, Paris, http://dx.doi.org/10.1787/5js69ld9w9nv-en.

- OECD (2013a), "Cities and Green Growth: The Case of the Chicago Tri-State Metropolitan Area", *OECD Regional Development Working Papers*, No. 2013/06, OECD Publishing, Paris, http://dx.doi.org/10.1787/5k49dv6c5xmv-en.

- OECD (2013b), "Urbanisation and Green Growth in China", OECD Regional Development Working Papers, No. 2013/07, *OECD Publishing*, Paris, http://dx.doi.org/10.1787/5k49dv68n7jf-en.

- Roy, R. (2014), "Environmental and Related Social Costs of the Tax Treatment of Company Cars and Commuting Expenses", *OECD Environment Working Papers*, No. 70, OECD Publishing, Paris, http://dx.doi.org/10.1787/5jxwrr5163zp-en.

- Ruijs, A. and H.R. Vollebergh (2013), "Lessons from 15 Years of Experience with the Dutch Tax Allowance for Energy Investments for Firms", *OECD Environment Working Papers*, No. 55, OECD Publishing, Paris, http://dx.doi.org/10.1787/5k47zw350q8v-en.

- Shogren, J. (2012), "Behavioural Economics and Environmental Incentives", *OECD Environment Working Papers*, No. 49, OECD Publishing, Paris, http://dx.doi.org/10.1787/5k8zwbhqs1xn-en.

- Silva, J., F. de Keulenaer and N. Johnstone (2012), "Environmental Quality and Life Satisfaction: Evidence Based on Micro-Data", *OECD Environment Working Papers*, No. 44, OECD Publishing, Paris, http://dx.doi.org/10.1787/5k9cw678dlr0-en.

- Wilson, L et al. (2014), "The Role of National Ecosystem Assessments in Influencing policy Making", *OECD Environment Working Papers*, No. 60, OECD Publishing, Paris, http://dx.doi.org/10.1787/5jxvl3zsbhkk-en.

Other OECD publications relevant to green growth

- Braconier, H., G. Nicoletti and B. Westmore (2014), "Policy Challenges for the Next 50 Years", *OECD Economic Policy Papers*, No. 9, OECD Publishing, Paris, http://dx.doi.org/10.1787/5jz18gs5fckf-en.
- Brandt, N., P. Schreyer and V. Zipperer (2013), "Productivity Measurement with Natural Capital", *OECD Economics Department Working Papers*, No. 1092, OECD Publishing, Paris, http://dx.doi.org/10.1787/5k3xnhsz0vtg-en.
- Criscuolo, C. and C. Menon (2014), "Environmental Policies and Risk Finance in the Green Sector: Cross-country Evidence", *OECD Science, Technology and Industry Working Papers*, No. 2014/01, OECD Publishing, Paris, http://dx.doi.org/10.1787/5jz6wn918j37-en.
- Criscuolo, C. et al. (2014), "Renewable Energy Policies and Cross-border Investment: Evidence from Mergers and Acquisitions in Solar and Wind Energy", *OECD Science, Technology and Industry Working Papers*, No. 2014/03, OECD, Paris, http://dx.doi.org/10.1787/5jxv9f3r9623-en.
- Criscuolo, C., P.N. Gal and C. Menon (2014), "The Dynamics of Employment Growth: New Evidence from 18 Countries", *OECD Science, Technology and Industry Policy Papers*, No. 14, OECD Publishing, Paris, http://dx.doi.org/10.1787/5jz417hj6hg6-en.
- G20/OECD (2012), "G20/OECD Policy Note on Pension Fund Financing for Green Infrastructure Initiatives", OECD Publishing, Paris, http://www.oecd.org/g20/topics/energy-environment-green-growth/S3%20G20%20OECD%20Pension%20funds%20for%20green%20infrastructure%20-%20June%202012.pdf.
- Gordon, K., J. Pohl and M. Bouchard (2014), "Investment Treaty Law, Sustainable Development and Responsible Business Conduct: A Fact Finding Survey", *OECD Working Papers on International Investment*, No. 2014/01, OECD Publishing, Paris, http://dx.doi.org/10.1787/5jz0xvgx1zlt-en.
- Harding, M. (2014), "Personal Tax Treatment of Company Cars and Commuting Expenses: Estimating the Fiscal and Environmental Costs", *OECD Taxation Working Papers*, No. 20, OECD Publishing, Paris, http://dx.doi.org/10.1787/5jz14cg1s7vl-en.
- IEA (2014a), Capturing the Multiple Benefits of Energy Efficiency: A Guide to Quantifying the Value Added, IEA, Paris, http://dx.doi.org/10.1787/9789264220720-en.
- IEA (2014b), *Energy Efficiency Market Report 2014*, IEA, Paris, http://dx.doi.org/10.1787/9789264218260-en.
- IEA (2014c), *Energy Technology Perspectives 2014, IEA*, Paris, http://dx.doi.org/10.1787/energy_tech-2014-en.
- IEA (2014d), *Medium-Term Renewable Energy Market Report 2014*, IEA, Paris, http://dx.doi.org/10.1787/renewmar-2014-en.
- IEA (2014e), *Tracking Clean Energy Progress 2014*, IEA, Paris, http://www.iea.org/etp/tracking/.
- IEA (2014f), *World Energy Outlook 2014*, IEA, Paris, http://dx.doi.org/10.1787/weo-2014-en.
- IEA (2013), *World Energy Outlook 2013*, IEA, Paris, http://dx.doi.org/10.1787/weo-2013-en.
- IEA (2012), *World Energy Outlook 2012*, IEA, Paris, http://dx.doi.org/10.1787/weo-2012-en.
- OECD/ITF (2015), *ITF Transport Outlook 2015*, OECD Publishing, Paris/ITF, Paris, http://dx.doi.org/10.1787/9789282107782-en.
- Miranda, G. and G. Larcombe (2012), "Enabling Local Green Growth: Addressing Climate Change Effects on Employment and Local Development", *OECD Local Economic and Employment Development (LEED) Working Papers*, No. 2012/01, OECD Publishing, Paris, http://dx.doi.org/10.1787/5k9h2q92t2r7-en.

- OECD, AfDB, United Nations and World Bank (N.D.), "A Toolkit of Policy Options to Support Inclusive Green Growth: Submission to the G20 Development Working Group", OECD, Paris, www.oecd.org/media/oecdorg/directorates/developmentco-operationdirectoratedcd-dac/environmentanddevelopment/IGG-ToolkitAfDB-OECD-UN-WB-revised_July_2013.pdf.
- OECD (forthcoming a), "Policy Framework for Investment, 2015", Chapter 13, OECD Publishing, Paris.
- OECD (forthcoming b), "Aligning Policies for the Transition to a Low-Carbon Economy", OECD Publishing, Paris, http://dx.doi.org/10.1787/9789264233294-en.
- OECD (forthcoming c), "Biodiversity offsets: Effective Design and Implementation", OECD Publishing, Paris.
- OECD (forthcoming d), "Overcoming Barriers to International Investment in Clean Energy", OECD Publishing, Paris, http://dx.doi.org/10.1787/9789264227064-en.
- OECD (forthcoming e), "Economic Policy Reforms 2015: Going for Growth", Chapter 4, OECD Publishing, Paris, http://dx.doi.org/10.1787/growth-2015-en.
- OECD (forthcoming h), "Principles on Water Governance for the Meeting of the Council at Ministerial Level 2015", OECD, Paris.
- OECD (forthcoming j), "Update on the OECD's Work on Climate Finance and Investment for the Meeting of the Council at Ministerial Level, 2015", OECD, Paris.
- OECD/ITF (forthcoming), "Aligning Policies to Favour Low-Carbon Transport", OECD Publishing/ITF, Paris.
- OECD/ITF (2013), *Better Regulation of Public-Private Partnerships for Transport Infrastructure, ITF Round Tables*, No. 151, OECD Publishing, Paris/ITF, Paris, http://dx.doi.org/10.1787/9789282103951-en.
- OECD (2015), *Water Resources Allocation: Sharing Risks and Opportunities, OECD Studies on Wate*r, OECD Publishing, Paris, http://dx.doi.org/10.1787/9789264229631-en.
- OECD (2014a), *Climate Resilience in Development Planning: Experiences in Colombia and Ethiopia*, OECD Publishing, Paris, http://dx.doi.org/10.1787/9789264209503-en.
- OECD (2014b), "Creating an environment for investment and sustainable development", in OECD, Development Co-operation Report 2014: Mobilising Resources for Sustainable Development, OECD Publishing, Paris, http://dx.doi.org/10.1787/dcr-2014-16-en.
- OECD (2014c), "Finding Synergies for Environment and Development Finance", in OECD, *Development Co-operation Report 2014: Mobilising Resources for Sustainable Development*, OECD Publishing, Paris, http://dx.doi.org/10.1787/dcr-2014-22-en.
- OECD (2014d), *Greening Household Behaviour: Overview from the 2011 Survey - Revised edition*, OECD Studies on Environmental Policy and Household Behaviour, OECD Publishing, Paris, http://dx.doi.org/10.1787/9789264214651-en.
- OECD (2014e), *How's Life in Your Region? Measuring Regional and Local Well-being for Policy Makin*g, OECD Publishing, Paris, http://dx.doi.org/10.1787/9789264217416-en.
- OECD (2014f), "Innovating to finance development", in *Development Co-operation Report 2014: Mobilising Resources for Sustainable Development*, OECD Publishing, Paris, http://dx.doi.org/10.1787/dcr-2014-19-en.
- OECD (2014g), *Job Creation and Local Economic Development*, OECD Publishing, Paris, http://dx.doi.org/10.1787/9789264215009-en.

- OECD (2014h), *Nanotechnology and Tyres: Greening Industry and Transport*, OECD Publishing, Paris, http://dx.doi.org/10.1787/9789264209152-en.
- OECD (2014i), *The Cost of Air Pollution: Health Impacts of Road Transport*, OECD Publishing, Paris, http://dx.doi.org/10.1787/9789264210448-en.
- OECD (2014j), *Water Governance in the Netherlands: Fit for the Future?* OECD Studies on Water, OECD Publishing, Paris, http://dx.doi.org/10.1787/9789264102637-en.
- OECD (2013k), *Long-Term Investors and Green Infrastructure: Policy Highlights*, OECD Publishing, Paris, www.oecd.org/env/cc/Investors%20in%20Green%20Infrastructure%20brochure%20(f)%20[lr].pdf.
- OECD (2013l), *Scaling-up Finance Mechanisms for Biodiversity*, OECD Publishing, Paris, http://dx.doi.org/10.1787/9789264193833-en.
- OECD (2013m), *Taxing Energy Use: A Graphical Analysis*, OECD Publishing, Paris, http://dx.doi.org/10.1787/9789264183933-en.
- OECD (2013n), "Stakeholder Meeting April 2013: The Future of the Ocean Economy: Exploring the Prospects for emerging ocean industries to 2030", OECD, Paris.
- OECD (2013o), "Workshop on Global Value Chains in Shipbuilding, Presentation on The Future of the Ocean Economy: Exploring the prospects for emerging ocean industries to 2030", An OECD/IFP Foresight Project, http://www.oecd.org/sti/ind/Barrie%20Stevens%20OECD.pdf.
- OECD (2012a), "An OECD-Wide Inventory of Support to Fossil-Fuel Production or Use", OECD, Paris, http://www.oecd.org/site/tadffss/Fossil%20Fuels%20Inventory_Policy_Brief.pdf.
- OECD (2012b), *OECD Employment Outlook 2012*, OECD Publishing, Paris, http://dx.doi.org/10.1787/empl_outlook-2012-en.
- OECD (2012c), *Energy and Climate Policy: Bending the Technological Trajectory*, OECD Studies on Environmental Innovation, OECD Publishing, Paris, http://dx.doi.org/10.1787/9789264174573-en.
- OECD (2012d), "Executive summary", in OECD, Meeting the Water Reform Challenge, OECD Publishing, Paris, http://dx.doi.org/10.1787/9789264170001-3-en.
- OECD (2012e), *Greening Development: Enhancing Capacity for Environmental Management and Governance*, OECD Publishing, Paris, http://dx.doi.org/10.1787/9789264167896-en.
- OECD (2012f), *Mortality Risk Valuation in Environment, Health and Transport Policies*, OECD Publishing, Paris, http://dx.doi.org/10.1787/9789264130807-en.
- OECD (2012g), OECD Environmental Outlook to 2050: The Consequences of Inaction, OECD Publishing, Paris, http://dx.doi.org/10.1787/9789264122246-en.
- OECD (2012h), "Proposal for a Project on: The Future of the Ocean Economy: Exploring the Prospects for emerging ocean industries to 2030".
- OECD (2012i), *Rebuilding Fisheries: The Way Forward*, OECD Publishing, Paris, http://dx.doi.org/10.1787/9789264176935-en.
- OECD (2012j), Sustainable Materials Management: Making Better Use of Resources, OECD Publishing, Paris. DOI: http://dx.doi.org/10.1787/9789264174269-en.
- OECD (2009), *Declaration on Green Growth, adopted at the OECD Council Meeting at Ministerial level on 25 June 2009*, www.oecd.org/officialdocuments/publicdisplaydocumentpdf/?doclanguage=en&cote=C/MIN(2009)5/ADD1/FINAL.

Other OECD publications relevant to green growth

- Bowen, A. and C. Hepburn (2014), "Green Growth", *Oxford Review of Economic Policy*, Vo. 30(3), http://oxrep.oxfordjournals.org/content/current.
- European Commission (2011), "Proposal for a Council Directive Amending Directive 2003/96/EC Restructuring the Community Framework for the Taxation of Energy Products and Electricity", http://eur-lex.europa.eu/LexUriServ/LexUriServ.do?uri=OJ:L:2003:283:0051:0070:EN:PDF.
- Kennedy, C and J. Corfee-Morlot (2013), "Past performance and future needs for low carbon climate resilient infrastructure – an investment perspective", http://dx.doi.org/10.1016/j.enpol.2013.04.031.
- The New Climate Economy (2014), The New Climate Economy Report, http://newclimateeconomy.report/.
- TNO (2013), *Kansen voor een circulaire economie in Nederland* [Opportunities for a circular economy in the Netherlands"], TNO, Delft, http://www.rijksoverheid.nl/bestanden/documenten-en-publicaties/rapporten/2013/06/20/tno-rapport-kansen-voor-de-circulaire-economie-in-nederland/tno-rapport-kansen-voor-de-circulaire-economie-in-nederland.pdf.
- The White House, Office of the Press Secretary (November 11, 2014), *U.S.-China Joint Announcement on Climate Change*, www.whitehouse.gov/the-press-office/2014/11/11/us-china-joint-announcement-climate-change.
- World Bank and Ecofys (2014), *State and trends of carbon pricing 2014*, World Bank Group, Washington, DC, http://documents.worldbank.org/curated/en/2014/05/19572833/state-trends-carbon-pricing-2014.
- World Economic Forum (2012), *The Green Investment Report: the ways and means to unlock private finance for green growth*, World Economic Forum Publishing, Geneva, http://www3.weforum.org/docs/WEF_GreenInvestment_Report_2013.pdf.

ORGANISATION FOR ECONOMIC CO-OPERATION AND DEVELOPMENT

The OECD is a unique forum where governments work together to address the economic, social and environmental challenges of globalisation. The OECD is also at the forefront of efforts to understand and to help governments respond to new developments and concerns, such as corporate governance, the information economy and the challenges of an ageing population. The Organisation provides a setting where governments can compare policy experiences, seek answers to common problems, identify good practice and work to co-ordinate domestic and international policies.

The OECD member countries are: Australia, Austria, Belgium, Canada, Chile, the Czech Republic, Denmark, Estonia, Finland, France, Germany, Greece, Hungary, Iceland, Ireland, Israel, Italy, Japan, Korea, Luxembourg, Mexico, the Netherlands, New Zealand, Norway, Poland, Portugal, the Slovak Republic, Slovenia, Spain, Sweden, Switzerland, Turkey, the United Kingdom and the United States. The European Union takes part in the work of the OECD.

OECD Publishing disseminates widely the results of the Organisation's statistics gathering and research on economic, social and environmental issues, as well as the conventions, guidelines and standards agreed by its members.

OECD PUBLISHING, 2, rue André-Pascal, 75775 PARIS CEDEX 16
(97 2015 07 1 P) ISBN 978-92-64-23441-3 – 2015

www.ingramcontent.com/pod-product-compliance
Lightning Source LLC
LaVergne TN
LVHW081417110826
845149LV00010B/1777